Sexual Repression and Victorian Literature

Sexual Repression and Victorian Literature

Russell M. Goldfarb, 1934-

Lewisburg
BUCKNELL UNIVERSITY PRESS

Library of Congress Catalogue Card Number: 70–101685

Associated University Presses, Inc.
Cranbury, New Jersey 08512

SBN 8387 7619 1
Printed in the United States of America

for my mother and father
and to Clare

Contents

Preface

Late Victorian literature, especially the literature of estheticism and decadence, was sexually expressive: from Swinburne to Arthur Symons, from Pater to Oscar Wilde, there are about three decades in the nineteenth century when writers were openly concerned with sex, sin, and sensual pleasures. During these years, novelists and poets did not deal exclusively with sexuality, but they did at times write frankly and with candor about debauchery, sexual immorality, and perversity. They wrote about these things, in part, because they were reacting against the moral demands and against the artistically constrictive atmosphere of the earlier decades in the century.

Sociologists and historians tell us that the early and mid-Victorian age was sexually repressive; psychologists, however, tell us that individuals, if not consciously, will unconsciously find ways of expressing their ostensibly repressed sexual energies. Here, then, is a context for literature: the critic can place a novel or poem in the perspectives offered by what he knows of Victorian sexual morality and the psychology of sexual repression. This book asks and attempts to answer the question, "How did novels and poems written in a sexually repressive age express sexuality?"

The literature which chiefly concerns me was written almost exclusively during the period bracketed by the First Reform Bill of 1832 and the Second Reform Bill of 1867. I find that different kinds of disguised sexuality inform specific poems of Robert Browning, Alfred Tennyson, and the Spasmodic school of poets; disguised sexuality also informs novels by Charles Dickens, Charlotte Brontë, and George Meredith. The present work analyzes more than a dozen nineteenth-century novels and poems which, in a variety of ways, treat subjects such as intercourse, frigidity, voyeurism, masturbation, homosexuality, and incest.

Before approaching the literary essays in the following pages, many readers will want to refer to the material of Chapter 1, "Victorian Sexual Morality," and the general reader is strongly urged to read next, in the Appendix, "The Dynamics of Sexual Repression." This review of Freudian psychology establishes a key premise of my book: when the unconscious mind tries to contain repressed sexual energy, that energy drives constantly for release through expressive outlets, and those outlets can be identified by the trained observer. The sexual dimension, the sexual depth, of Victorian literature has yet to be fully explored, but the psychologically oriented reader who knows how repressed sexuality makes itself manifest is in a position to help further that exploration.

An early version of my chapter on "The Last Ride Together" appeared in *Victorian Poetry,* and I would like to thank the editors for permission to incorporate the essay in this book. A selection from the chapter on Tennyson was read as a paper before the language and literature section of the Michigan Academy of Science, Arts, and Letters.

To many faculty and staff members of Western Michigan University I am grateful for assistance; a sabbatical leave and a reduced teaching load gave me time to write, and a grant from the Faculty Research Fund helped financially.

Many of my graduate students gave helpful suggestions and research assistance. I especially want to acknowledge the help of Sybil Myers Combs, Harriet Dye, Janice Davis Lee, and Ken Patterson.

Among my colleagues in the English department, I am thankful first to Clare Goldfarb, who gave welcome aid and comfort in addition to professional assistance. John Phillips read my manuscript closely and gave valuable criticism with regard to content and style. For help through all stages of preparing this book I cannot adequately thank Frederick Rogers.

Acknowledgments

I would like to thank the following publishers for permission to quote from copyrighted material:

Basic Books, Inc., for permission to quote from Steven Marcus, *The Other Victorians,* 1966.

Cornell University Press, for permission to quote from Taylor Stoehr, *The Dreamer's Stance,* 1965.

Harcourt, Brace, and World, Inc., for permission to quote from David Magarshack, *Dostoevsky,* 1963.

Harvard University Press, for permission to quote from Jerome H. Buckley, *The Victorian Temper,* 1951.

W. W. Norton and Company, Inc., for permission to quote from Otto Fenichel, *The Psychoanalytic Theory of Neurosis,* 1945. I also acknowledge a permission granted by Routledge and Kegan Paul Ltd.

The University of Chicago Press, for permission to quote from Richard D. Altick, *The English Common Reader,* 1963.

Sigmund Freud Copyrights Ltd., the Institute of Psycho-Analysis and the Hogarth Press Ltd., for permission to quote from the Standard Edition of the *Complete Psychological Works of Sigmund Freud,* revised and edited by James Strachey, 1953-1966. I also acknowledge publishing rights held by Allen and Unwin Ltd. for *Introductory Lectures on Psycho-Analysis;* W. W. Norton, Inc. for *The Ego and the Id* and *An Autobiographical Study;* and I thank Basic Books, Inc., for permission to quote from *Three Essays on the Theory of Sexuality,* translated and newly edited by James Strachey (1962) and from Volume 5 of *The Collected Papers of Sigmund Freud,* edited by Ernest Jones, M.D. (1959).

Sexual Repression and Victorian Literature

I
Victorian Sexual Morality

I

The game of historical voyeurism has simple rules. A player first chooses an era—any era will do—and then he titillates himself and his audience by describing all of the sexual objects and acts which he can imaginatively relate to the age. Historical voyeurism is a game, a playful mental contest, because the serious, disciplined search for truth is never at issue. Depending upon his mental prowess, one merely finds in history what he is capable of putting there. And history is obliging, for she accepts any and all variations or aberrations of human sexual behavior. If sodomists can be discovered in Sussex today, they could have been discovered there three hundred years ago. If nudity is displayed in twentieth-century London, then research can easily prove it was displayed in medieval London. But the fact remains that historical voyeurism is a game, even a pernicious game.

It is pernicious to scholarship, for it undermines the serious attempt to place the sexual tone of an age in historical perspective. When any kind of behavior can be found at any time in history, then there is no perspective. And yet sexual history is obviously not of a kind from one age to the next. Elizabethan England differed from Cromwell's England just as Victorian England differed from modern England. The key difference between the voyeuristic games that people play and the history which scholars write is a matter of selectivity. For example, the gamesman who chooses the Victorian era selects to describe nineteenth-century pornography, or prostitution, or flagellation societies. He ignores the dominant sexual culture of the age in order to describe its subculture. By the same token, one might just as easily choose the most licentious age in history and select to describe its puritan characteristics. History will indulge the games that people play.

But scholars select in order to establish general characteristics. The spirit of an age, *Zeitgeist,* cultural tone—these are academic catchwords meant to call to mind broad, truthful pictures of a society taken whole. Selectivity works here to focus an image, not to distort it. One seeks the typical, not the atypical; the characteristic, not the uncharacteristic. The paradox of scholarship and gamesmanship is that both are judged, both are evaluated by the success or failure of the kind of selectivity which is used. The means become as important as their ends.

The end toward which these pages are directed is to show the principal features of early and mid-Victorian sexual morality. What will emerge is the portrait of an age which was importantly shaped by powers that served to repress sexual expression. The means used to draw this portrait are various; they include discussions of sanctions in areas religious, political, legal, economic, and domestic. A common denominator to all of the sanctions is the extraordinarily repressive sexual conduct demanded by Victorian society. And here is where selectivity operates: in order to create a truthful picture of an age which was intent on discouraging sexual permissiveness, one must concentrate on those forces in society which helped to create the dominant sexual tone. That means for the time being the sexual subculture of Victorian England must be ignored, even though its sexual violence and variety were historically real. Some attention will be given to this subculture in order to present an undistorted history, but again one must select to show that the Victorian scale was heavily, heavily weighted on the side of sexual inhibition.

In present-day London, London of the 1960's, there is a high degree of sexual permissiveness. To report on the general public's tolerance of sexuality, one must select to write about expression rather than repression even though repressive forces are everywhere present in English life. The point is that even the casual observer, the ordinary tourist, will quickly become aware of sexual display in public life. The dominant sexual nature of what *Time* magazine has called "Swinging London" is for both casual and scholarly observer remarkably uninhibited. The balance is weighted by evidence which is conspicuously present.

Young women call attention to their sexuality by wearing miniskirts, tight sweaters, tight pants, low-cut gowns, and transparent dresses. In appropriate circumstances the general public allows young women to wear bikinis and monokinis. Beauty contestants in scanty dress are commonplace, and performers without dress appear regularly in Soho burlesque houses. These are no longer night clubs, for the houses frequently open, and strip shows start, at noon. Store mannequins and advertisement models display brassieres, panties, and girdles. Full-color posters of men and women in undergarments line the escalator paths to underground trains. Bookstalls display calendar art, health and sunbather magazines which feature nudity, literature with erotic content, and magazines which exploit perversions. Commercial advertisements for books and movies exploit their sexual content. Language is uninhibited in books, films, and theater. *Blow-Up* and *Marat de Sade* made displays of nudity possible in movies and on the legitimate stage. Sexual scandals are given detailed coverage by newspapers, radio, and television. Museums contain pop and op art works whose subjects are frequently male and female nudes treated with the frankest kind of realism. The general public tolerates these expressions of sexuality, most of which are visual, all of which combine to form a public image of present-day London.

Whether the public image of London coincides with its citizens' private image of their city is a moot point. The average person, the man in the street, may privately deplore his society's sexual mores, but he willingly allows a corporate image to say he is extremely permissive and tolerant of sexual expression. During the early to mid-Victorian age, say one hundred to one hundred and thirty-five years ago, this same man, individually and in concert with the vast majority of his countrymen, wanted his public image, above all else, to be respectable. In matters of sex, this meant purity, wholesomeness, and virtue. This meant the look he presented to the world, the look he desperately wanted history to preserve, was to be pre-eminently moral. Descriptive of his sexual conduct are words such as inhibited, restrained, and repressed.

Sexual expression in the Victorian age was carefully controlled. The number of controlling agencies and the intensity with which they did their work was so formidable that the very word "Victorian" has come to have its unique sexual meaning. A standard dictionary will define the word as relating to Queen Victoria or to her reign and then define Victorian morality as though the single adjective were really a compound word. A typical secondary meaning has the word "pertaining to or characteristic of the ideals and standards of morality and taste prevalent during the reign of Queen Victoria; prudish; conventional; narrow." One of the grand ironies of history is that an age tremendously concerned with repressing its sexual activity has become known as an age to be described by its sexual mores. The truth is, of course, the Victorian age was obsessed with hiding sex, and this obsession accounts for the extraordinary pressures the age brought to bear upon society to satisfy its compulsion. If sexual expression could be hidden deeply enough, if it could be successfully repressed, completely repressed, then one could speak easily and apparently without guilt of being respectable.

One sign of respectability was an involvement with the Church, for the Church promised to regulate morality. Religious life in Victorian England was supremely important. As Jerome Buckley says, "The early and mid-Victorians were wonderfully concerned with religious controversy and ethical debate; and the reading of sermons was perhaps the most popular of their literary pastimes."[1] Religious involvement was popular at least through the middle of the century when the combination of scientific findings (primarily by the geologist Charles Lyell and the naturalist Charles Darwin) and the religious findings of the Higher Criticism (Strauss, Renan) finally gathered enough force after years of coming together to make comfortable religious belief impossible. But as long as belief was comfortable, the Victorians undoubtedly believed in, talked about, and joined an acceptable life of religious fellowship. The Census report of 1851-1853 noted, "The middle classes have augmented rather than diminished that devotional sentiment and strictness of attention to religious services by which, for several centuries, they have so eminently been distinguished. With the upper classes, too, the subject of religion has obtained of late a marked degree of notice, and a regular church attendance is now ranked among the recognized proprieties of life."[2] The lower classes could not always afford the proprieties of life, but religion was in reach of all, and the poor had not even to reach. Religion came to them—

from the landowner in the country, from the factory owner in the city; from rural missionaries and from urban workers-among-the-poor. Of importance is the kind of religion which came to them.

The Anglican Church at the start of the Victorian age claimed allegiance from the vast majority of professed Christians. The stern religious attitude toward English morality, however, was formed a generation earlier not by high Anglicans in an established church, but by low church Evangelicals and groups of Methodists who had been expelled from the State church in the reign of George III. Although leaders of the Evangelical movement were dead by the time Victoria ascended the throne (William Wilberforce and Hannah More died in 1833), the movement was a fountainhead of repressive forces which swamped the nineteenth century.

Born and raised in an Evangelical era and in various ways affected by its repressive forces were writers such as Thomas Carlyle (1795), Thomas Macaulay (1800), John Henry Newman (1801), Harriet Martineau (1802), Elizabeth Barrett (1806), Alfred Tennyson (1809), Elizabeth Gaskell (1810), William Thackeray (1811), Charles Dickens (1812), Robert Browning (1812), Anthony Trollope (1815), Charlotte Brontë (1816), Emily Brontë (1818), George Eliot (1819), Charles Kingsley (1819), John Ruskin (1819). As late as 1834 the Evangelical movement was still strong enough to virtually change George Eliot's way of life. Gordon Haight relates the story in an introduction to his edition of *Adam Bede*:

> The all-absorbing interest of her [Marian Evans'] early life was religion. Brought up in the easygoing, unquestioning branch of the Church of England . . . , at the age of fifteen she was profoundly impressed by the Evangelical movement; from then until her twenty-second year her life was dominated by an almost painful piety. She taught Sunday school

> classes, visited poor cottagers, organized clothing clubs and charities of all kinds; she cultivated ascetic habits, dressing with unbecoming plainness and frowning on worldly pleasures, however innocent.[3]

People from all walks of life grew up under Evangelical training and then as adults in Victorian England they responded to a morality inculcated in childhood. For example, the captains of industry in the 1830's, the new mill owners and factory owners who as children sang Wesleyan hymns in the rural or urban chapel, would as grown men move among lathes and spinning mules urging their workers to serve the Church, to save their souls, to discipline their lives. Religion was straight, narrow, and terrifying.

Early in the narrative of Emily Brontë's *Wuthering Heights* Mr. Lockwood tells of a nightmare in which he hears a sermon delivered by the Reverend Jabes Branderham in the Chapel of Gimmerden Sough: "Jabes had a full and attentive congregation: and he preached—good God—what a sermon! Divided into *four hundred and ninety* parts—each fully equal to an ordinary address from the pulpit—and each discussing a separate sin!" The Evangelical ideal was unremittingly severe. George Burden's *Sermon on Lawful Amusements* (1804) was hardly extreme in urging that Sundays be devoted exclusively to God, even to the banning of travel and the practice of paying afternoon social visits. Of course blasphemy was prohibited, but it was as inclusively defined as prostitution, which referred to all extramarital sexual experience. John Wesley had advised his followers to avoid all manners of passions, and this led in the early nineteenth century to the inhibition of spontaneity and the suspicion of all emotional expression which was not explicitly directed to church service. Fervent display was limited to watch nights, band meetings, and revivalist campaigns.

It was not at all tolerated in courtship, flirtation, or in any of the traditional forms of sexual expression.

After careful study of Methodism, mainly from 1790-1830, Edward Palmer Thompson concluded in *The Making of the English Working Class,* "Methodism is permeated with teachings as to the sinfulness of sexuality, and as to the extreme sinfulness of the sexual organs. These—and especially the male sexual organs (since it became increasingly the convention that women could not feel the 'lust of the flesh') —were the visible fleshly citadels of Satan."[4] In the mind of an evangelizing Methodist, the only sexual activity permissible was conjugal intercourse for the purpose of procreation.

Sexual promiscuity was a heinous sin, but so was the giving of pleasure parties on a Sunday, the Lord's day. Somewhat less wicked, nevertheless sinful, was neglecting private prayer, reading novels, getting drunk, or going to the theater. "Thou shalt not" may indeed have prefaced four hundred and ninety separate sins in Evangelical sermons, hymns, diaries, tracts, prayerbooks, weeklies, and throwaways. The message was spread in church preaching, street-corner preaching, preaching in the fields, prayer meetings, and in house-to-house calls.

Moral injunctions were also widely publicized in religious literature, the largest catalogue of publications in nineteenth-century England. Bible publication became an industry with no lack of audience among the mass reading public. Richard D. Altick observed:

> Religious literature . . . was everywhere in nineteenth-century England. Tracts were flung from carriage windows; they were passed out at railway stations; they turned up in army camps and in naval vessels anchored in the roads, and in jails and lodging houses and hospitals and workhouses; they were distributed in huge quantities at Sunday and day schools, as rewards for punctuality, diligence, decorum, and deloused heads. They were a ubiquitous part of the social landscape.[5]

Evangelical Anglicans and dissenting Methodists left as a legacy to the Victorian age a stern morality which was especially repressive in all areas of sexual behavior. It remained for the age to prosecute its legacy.

The law was an obvious means of regulating morality. Various petty moral offenses were given legal attention and an eighteenth-century Royal Proclamation Against Vice was invoked to prohibit Victorians from playing games on Sunday, in public or private, and from selling alcoholic beverages during periods of church services. In 1789 a Proclamation Society was formed to lobby for enforcement of the Royal Proclamation; this society in 1803 formed the Society for the Suppression of Vice, a group which became extremely active arguing for legal restraints during Victoria's reign. Other groups lobbying for moral legislation and for strict enforcement of existing legislation were the Association for Securing a Better Observance of Sunday, the Society for the Prevention of Female Prostitution, and the Religious Tract Society. By 1844 this latter group was publishing fifteen million tracts a year.

These groups were primarily effective in influencing the social conscience of the age, and only sporadically successful in influencing parliamentary legislation. In 1800, 1856, and again in 1857 reformers tried to get Parliament to legislate the death sentence for adultery, an example of the extreme to which they were driven by righteous indignation. They did get Parliament to pass one of the more laughable laws of the nineteenth century, an act which banned marriage with a deceased wife's sister. (The act went unrepealed until 1907.) Not laughable was the zeal with which reformers urged social and legal restraints upon matters of both major and minor importance.

Information about contraceptive devices was suppressed

on moral grounds. Section four of the Vagrancy Act of 1824 was vigorously upheld, a section that provides, " 'Every person wilfully, openly, lewdly and obscenely exposing his person with intent to insult any female' is a rogue and vagabond. . . . On second conviction as a rogue or vagabond the offender may be committed to Quarter Sessions for sentence as an incorrigible rogue." Exposure was an offense serious enough to warrant more than one sanction. At common law, the offense was not dependent upon intent to insult a female; here it was an indictable misdemeanor "publicly to exhibit the naked person or do any other act of open and notorious lewdness." Thus, exposure in the open part of a public urinal was a common-law offense. Under the Manchester Police Act of 1844, "every person shall be liable to a penalty of not more than forty shillings who in any street shall . . . wilfully and indecently expose his person."[6] These laws are not petty, but exposure was thought of more as an "act of open and notorious lewdness" than as a lesser affront to public decency. The difference in degree is a minor indication of the moral posture of the age.

Since laws are subject to interpretation, it is rarely the law itself which engenders moral severity. Parliament in 1843 passed the Theatres Act, a statute which attempted to regulate the performance of stage plays specifically to prevent riot or misbehavior, but which also empowered the Lord Chamberlain to close any theatre on such public occasions as he should think fitting. The fact that the Lord Chamberlain was legally empowered to determine the relevancy of the Theatres Act at any given time was itself morally suasive.

The power of legal interpretation, with particular reference to England's obscenity laws, became the subject of parliamentary controversy in the mid-nineteenth century. Backed by the Society for the Suppression of Vice,

Lord Chief Justice Campbell urged Parliament in the 1850's to strengthen an 1824 law which made it an offense to display obscene books and prints in public. Transcripts show the House of Lords hotly debated the subject, but the Lords were joined by members of the House of Commons in 1857 to pass the Obscene Publications Act. The act gave police and justices of the peace authority to confiscate and destroy obscene literature; supporters of the act hoped to prevent not only sales but also the publication of obscene literature. Lord Campbell assured his peers the act would be used solely against gross pornography: it was to apply to works "written with the single purpose of corrupting the morals of youth and of a nature calculated to shock the feeling of decency in any well-regulated mind."[7] Quality literature was to be unaffected, and a book such as Alexandre Dumas fils' *La Dame aux Camélias,* then popular in England, would not be banned. (In 1850, the authorities permitted the opera *La Traviata* to be performed, but they forbade the translation of the libretto into English text.) By 1868, eleven years after passage of the Obscene Publications Act, there was new interpretation of the act: Lord Chief Justice Alexander Cockburn said, "I think the test of obscenity is this, whether the tendency of the matter charged as obscenity is to deprave and corrupt those whose minds are open to such immoral influences, and into whose hands a publication of this sort may fall." This definition was printed in textbooks and accepted as the official interpretation of the 1857 act. Not the act, but its interpretation served years later to ban Émile Zola's *La Terre* and James Joyce's *Ulysses.*

Fear of government regulations, of bureaucratic authority in legal areas of interpretation and enforcement, explains British caution in passing laws to regulate morality. Individual liberties seemed less threatened by social sanctions than by legal sanctions. Victorians quietly accepted a common-law prohibition against the keeping of brothels, but it was not until 1866 that Parliament passed the Contagious Diseases Act, an attempt to control the hygienics of prostitutes by making them have periodic medical examinations at health stations strategically located near army encampments and naval stations. The act was soon repealed because of pressure from people who spoke continuously of the dangers of legally restricting individual liberty. A review of the quantity and quality of moral legislation passed during the early and mid-Victorian age shows that Parliament did not shape but in a relatively minor way contributed to the sexually repressive character of the times. Religious groups were far more important in establishing the Victorian moral disposition, and law was at times useful in helping to sustain that disposition.

It was useful, for example, as a weapon to those who favored moral censorship. If community pressures to censor objectionable materials were unsuccessful, there was always the threat of taking a particular case to court. Ordinarily, the threat was unnecessary. Evangelical denominations had worked for decades to promote wholesomeness in literature, and they not only guarded society from sexually offensive publications, but they warned against all imaginative literature that was not patently Christian and pure in purpose and effect. Religious literature was readily available, socially acceptable, and usually free. Morally questionable material was still available, never free, and socially frowned upon. The Butterly Coal Company distributed Bibles to its workers, who were urged to read only that literature which would help to form their Christian character. Evangelical missionaries canvassed homes to promote tastes for religious reading.

Guardians of morality in literature made their case at church, at work, or in the home. Thus, the proscription of non-Christian literature was well publicized.

A number of organized societies were also on guard. The Constitutional Association was particularly interested in prosecuting seditious works, among which they included Percy Bysshe Shelley's *Queen Mab* and *Oedipus Tyrannus;* in spirit its members were kin to members of the Society for the Suppression of Vice. The targets of this society were blasphemous and impure books, obscene publications, and off-color song sheets and books. The Society for Pure Literature had a self-explanatory name, but the Society for the Diffusion of Useful Knowledge needs comment.

The Useful Knowledge proponents were Utilitarians, an essentially political body that had a great deal to say about reading habits in the Victorian age. The Utilitarians were in many ways as powerful a moral force as the Evangelicals. Their ultimate aim was to develop a healthy society by appealing to the reason of men to pursue practical ends in life by practical means. Imaginative literature was impractical because it served no demonstrably useful purpose. Sexual expression was impractical because it diverted men from work, it appealed to emotion rather than to reason, and it did nothing to further the progress of society. Procreation was meaningful; all other forms of sexuality were, practically speaking, merely a waste of precious time. Reading time could be profitably spent on books on self-improvement. There were trade manuals to learn, new methods of agriculture to read about, economic theories to digest; there were also mill, factory, mine, and farm efficiency plans to keep abreast of. Utilitarian literature was, as the name suggests, a literature of utility. Books, pamphlets, journals, and magazines were used by the Evangelicals for the religious welfare of England; they were used by the Utilitarians for the business welfare of England.

Under the influence of two pre-Victorian men, John Wesley and Jeremy Bentham, religious and political bodies joined in the early and mid-nineteenth century to define respectability in literature. In overt and subtle ways they helped to censor the reading materials of a population that by 1861 had reached twenty millions of people. Flooding the market with their publications affected potential readers simply by making those publications readily available. Schoolroom literature for children of the middle and upper classes was affected by the Evangelical and Utilitarian spirit, for education was in the hands of those who fully supported purity and progress, morality and utility, wholesomeness and self-improvement. Victorian novelists and poets were not studied in boarding schools, day schools, public schools, or grammar schools. The universities still concentrated on Greek and Latin literature, and not until the close of the century did they become officially aware of contemporary literature. Byron and Dickens, Keats and Eliot had to be read after hours, at home, or on vacation. They were read by thousands of self-taught people among the lower and lower-middle classes, but the millions read religious and utilitarian literature, penny dreadfuls, and sensational weeklies. The point is, contemporary literature of quality had to make its way without encouragement from the school system and in spite of crusading vested-interest groups.

There is no question that it did successfully make its way; it is remarkable that in 1964 this statement could be made by a scholar such as William L. Burn, Professor of Modern History at King's College, University of Durham: "I have no doubt but that there was a higher proportion of the population who had read and were prepared to discuss the novels of Dickens and the poems of Tennyson than could be found to discuss the works of any particular novelist or poet today."[8] One needs to be reminded that Dicken's novels were frequently sold to over 30,000 buyers soon after publication; the first edition of Tennyson's *Idylls of the King* in 1859 ran to 40,000 copies, of which 10,000 sold the first week they were offered. Imaginative literature was supported in the marketplace, but the moral climate and restrictive conditions under which it was written have been only partially discussed. Even the threat of censorship was stronger than has been suggested by brief consideration of crusading Evangelicals, watchdog societies, and Utilitarians.

Many people suspected theatrical work of undermining morality, even as being inherently wicked in and of itself. Allardyce Nicoll discusses individual censors in *A History of Early Nineteenth Century Drama, 1800-1850* (1955), but generally speaking, Victorian suspicion of the theater was rooted in the puritan belief that stage plays were unsuitable and unlawful for Christians. An eighteenth-century Methodist minister, John Styles, declared it was "a luckless hour" when William Shakespeare decided to write for the stage, and in the nineteenth century Charlotte Brontë and George Eliot warned against impurities in Shakespeare. Thomas Bowdler believed one had only to purge the plays of their grossness in order to make them fit for family moral edification. Most early and mid-Victorians read their Shakespeare in Bowdler's 1818 edition, *The Family Shakespeare in Ten Volumes, in which nothing has been added to the original text, but those words and phrases are omitted which cannot with propriety be read in a family*. The subtitle of these volumes was as important as the title.

When Eric Partridge in 1948 published *Shakespeare's Bawdy* (the title is an abridgement of *Sexuality, Homo-*

sexuality, and Bawdiness in the Works of William Shakespeare), he noted in his Preface that the book could not have been published in the Victorian period. Indeed, Jerome Buckley notes in *The Victorian Temper,* "Francis Place, . . . reporting to the House of Commons on the improvement in public morals, produced evidence that books regarded as pornographic and illicit in the thirties had been freely advertised, displayed, and sold a generation earlier."[9] This pride in moral improvement through what amounts to literary censorship was largely the result of yet another publishing condition in Victorian England.

Publishers, editors, sometimes booksellers did not want to offend pressure groups or customers by dealing with morally questionable literature. Thus, only pure stories could appear, only pure novels could be serialized in magazines such as *Cornhill* or *Good Words.* Editors of these magazines paid generously for material they used; they could not afford the risk of losing circulation by offending the moral consciousness of large segments of their reading public. The publisher John Cassell had no better advertisement for the books he produced than his name on the spine, for Cassell had a widespread reputation as a temperance orator with the strictest of moral standards. In his vocation as publisher, Cassell was enormously successful: the *Working Man's Friend,* a penny publication, had a circulation of 50,000 the year after it began; *Cassell's Popular Educator* was annually a best seller; the *Illustrated Family Bible* sold 350,000 copies in six years. By 1862, Cassell had annual sales of 25 to 30 million copies of penny publications. When it came to publishing literary works, therefore, Cassell had a name to uphold, and he carefully chose what he published. As Richard D. Altick observed,

> Cassell's success was due both to a shrewd sense of popular taste and to the absolute blamelessness of the house's produc-

tions. Already associated in the popular mind with tea and temperance, the name of Cassell on a penny part or a cheap fireside paper was sufficient guarantee of its fitness for the strictest household. During Cassell's lifetime, at least, the pages of his publications were never sullied by mention of liquor.[10]

In his study of the Victorian book trade in *The English Common Reader,* Altick also called attention to the censorship activities of Charles Edward Mudie, the proprietor of the most influential circulating library in the eighteen fifties and sixties:

> By astute business methods, and above all by achieving a reputation as the watchdog of contemporary literary morals, Mudie did much to encourage reading among the class that could afford a guinea for a year's subscription. He throve upon the role of the mid-Victorian Mr. Grundy: "What will Mudie say?" was the invariable question that arose in publishers' offices when a new novel was under consideration. Mudie paid the piper, and on behalf of his large clientele he called the tune.

At mid-century, Mudie was so successful that in a decade's time he could order more than 400,000 copies of novels from various publishers. When he refused George Meredith's *The Ordeal of Richard Feverel* in 1859, his refusal curtailed the novel's earning power. Publishers wanting to recoup their financial investments in any given novel were naturally sensitive to the moral tastes of people such as Mudie. His largest competitor when ordering new books, W. H. Smith and Son, was equally censorious. William Henry Smith, Jr., was determined to woo people away from reading French novels in translation, sensational thrillers, and literary trash. He obtained a virtual monopoly of bookstalls at railway stations throughout England, and the only books he would offer for sale were those he considered morally respectable. W. H. Smith and

Son was as select as the house of Mudie when ordering novels. Tradesmen who controlled large retail outlets, therefore, could themselves censor literature by the practice and threat of applying economic sanctions to works they considered immoral. This kind of censorship was less direct than, say, overt listing in the Roman Catholic Index of prohibited reading, but it was as real.

There would be little point to listing all of the literature which Victorians felt was morally questionable when the examples of three works, each from the 1850's, each written by a woman, will serve to illustrate the kind of topic which was subject to stricture. First, there was *Ruth,* a novel by Mrs. Elizabeth Gaskell, published in 1853. The heroine, a lonely girl apprenticed to a milliner, is seduced by a minister who allows the girl to present herself as a widow with a legitimate son. Mrs. Gaskell's sympathies are with Ruth, but the reading public condemned a fallen woman as heroine and a minister in the role of a seducer. Second, Elizabeth Barrett Browning's 1857 novel in verse, *Aurora Leigh,* was roundly criticized for dealing too openly with the subject of an unmarried mother, and for referring indiscreetly to prostitution. George Eliot's *Adam Bede* (1859) was assailed for the teen-aged Hetty Sorrel's seduction by the young squire, Arthur Donnithorne. After she gives birth, Hetty leaves her child to die, and the immorality of this action was also criticized. *Adam Bede* was held to be "the vile outpourings of a lewd woman's mind," and the novel was withdrawn from circulating libraries by their righteous proprietors.

Safe literature neither depraved nor corrupted readers by treating immoral situations. It did not shock respectable women, and it did not offend their daughters. It held not the slightest tendency toward immoral constructions, nor did it make anyone question the proprieties of life. Safe literature supported the conventions, the beliefs, the mores of a society tremendously concerned with its front of respectability. The sexual beliefs upon which this front was built would today be characterized not by words such as "pure" or "wholesome," but by the words "naïve" or "unenlightened."

Sex was a secret in Victorian households. Fathers did not tell their sons the facts of life, nor did mothers tell their daughters. The family physician would not broach the subject; husbands and wives would not be open with one another. Many adult Victorians were completely ignorant about whole areas of human sexual behavior. The extent of sexual education in the early and mid-nineteenth-century respectable family was bound on one side by talk of chastity before marriage and bound on the other side by talk of fidelity after marriage. The ignorance of parents when raising their children, the desire to keep children sexually pure in mind and body, led to practices which hardly seem credible. There is a good deal of testimony, however, about such practices and one comes eventually to believe in their reality.

Consider, for example, what was done about masturbation. In *A History of Sexual Customs* (1958), Richard Lewinsohn writes, "Cages were manufactured which were fitted over a boy's genitals at night and carefully locked; some, for better protection, had spikes sticking out of them." G. Rattray Taylor found in *Sex in History* (1954) that the Victorians laid special stress on the dangers of masturbation and devoted immense care to its prevention. Preoccupation with the subject, Taylor wrote, began in Germany and spread to England:

> As early as 1786, in his *Unterricht für Eltern,* S. G. Vogel advocated the infibulation of the foreskin to prevent masturbation, and the subject became quite generally discussed in the first quarter of the nineteenth century. [In *Sexual Life in England, Past and Present* (1938)] I. Bloch speaks of

> small cages which fathers fitted to their sons, like a male girdle of chastity, keeping the key to themselves. J. L. Milton's book on the subject, *Spermatorrhea,* had run through twelve editions by 1887; he describes cages lined with spikes, which were worn at night, and even—grotesque thought—a device whereby any filial erection was made to ring an electric bell in the parent's room.

A Victorian physician, Dr. William Acton, wrote this about a boy who habitually masturbates:

> The frame is stunted and weak, the muscles undeveloped, the eye is sunken and heavy, the complexion is sallow, pasty, or covered with spots of acne, the hands are damp and cold, and the skin moist. The boy shuns the society of others, creeps about alone, joins with repugnance in the amusements of his schoolfellows. He cannot look any one in the face and becomes careless in dress and uncleanly in person. His intellect has become sluggish and enfeebled, and if his evil habits are persisted in, he may end in becoming a drivelling idiot or a peevish valetudinarian. Such boys are to be seen in all stages of degeneration, but what we have described is but the result towards which *they all* are tending.[11]

Masturbation in young men, according to Dr. Acton, will exhaust their vital forces and may well lead to mental disturbance. Aside from pornographers, neither Dr. Acton nor anyone else to my knowledge has written explicitly about masturbation among Victorian women, certainly because of a lack of information, probably because Victorians would not have admitted even to themselves that girls or women ever had the desire to masturbate. In 1966, Steven Marcus commented on the general acceptance among Victorians of the kinds of ideas here being discussed: "There can be little doubt that in this period of history we confront a situation characterized not merely by extreme disturbance and guilt over masturbation, and sexuality in general, but by the emergence of those feelings into general organized consciousness in the form of such beliefs."

Professor Marcus has valuable information on Victorian sexuality in *The Other Victorians* (New York: Basic Books, 1966). He studied the subject at the Kinsey Institute for Sex Research at Bloomington, Indiana, and there had the opportunity to work first-hand with various kinds of out-of-print rare materials. The first chapter of his book on sexuality and pornography in mid-nineteenth-century England is devoted primarily to the writings of Dr. William Acton. Other scholars have quoted briefly from Acton's work, but Marcus offers extensive paraphrases, summaries, and direct quotations from writings, primarily medical treatises, which "may be said to represent the official views of sexuality held by Victorian society—or, put in another way, the views held by the official culture." Even if one questions that assumption, there can be no disputing the desirability of having the sexual views of a learned Victorian physician.

From 1831 to 1836, Acton was an apprentice to the Resident Apothecary to St. Bartholomew's Hospital, London. He then went to Paris to study diseases of the urinary and generative organs, and served as an extern in the Female Venereal Hospital. In 1840, having returned to England, he was made a member of the Royal College of Surgeons. He became a Fellow of the Royal Medical and Chirurgical Society of London in 1842. Among his publications are *A Practical Treatise on Diseases of the Urinary and Generative Organs in Both Sexes* (1841); *Prostitution, Considered in Its Moral, Social, and Sanitary Aspects, in London and Other Large Cities and Garrison Towns, with Proposals for the Control and Prevention of Its Attendant Evils* (1857); *The Function and Disorders of the Reproductive Organs, in Childhood, Youth Adult Age, and Advanced Life, Considered in Their Physiological, Social and Moral Relations* (1857).

Years of study led Dr. Acton to the conclusion that

sexual behavior was directly related to physical and mental health. To be healthy in mind and body a person had to practice self-restraint; he had to control all sexual desires. Married men were particularly in danger of physiological deterioration unless they carefully regulated their sexual lives, for moderation, though not as beneficial as continence, was absolutely necessary for the preservation of health. An excerpt from a case history illustrates this belief:

> A medical man called on me, saying he found himself suffering from spermatorrhoea. There was general debility, inaptitude to work, disinclination for sexual intercourse, in fact, he thought he was losing his senses. The sight of one eye was affected. The only way in which he lost semen was, as he thought, by a slight occasional oozing from the penis. I asked him at once if he had ever committed excesses. As a boy, he acknowledged having abused himself, but he married seven years ago, being then a hearty, healthy man, and it was only lately that he had been complaining. In answer to my further inquiry, he stated that since his marriage he had had connection two or three times a week, and often more than once a night! This one fact, I was obliged to tell him, sufficiently accounted for all his troubles.

Sexual excess meant loss of sight and the fear of mental derangement to this patient; to others it could mean heart failure, loss of memory, a stunted frame, undeveloped muscles—in fact, it threatened all of the debilitating effects consequent to masturbation. The ideal Victorian health program had as rule number one the limiting of sexual intercourse as severely as possible.

This was no problem at all for women. "I should say that the majority of women (happily for them) are not very much troubled with sexual feeling of any kind." Dr. Acton says sexual feeling among loose, low, and vulgar women is exceptional and not to be found among the vast majority of women. Sadly exceptional are the insane women found in lunatic asylums who were victims of nymphomania. For the average woman, for the normal woman, it was a "vile aspersion" to say she was capable of sexual feeling. "As a general rule, a modest woman seldom desires any sexual gratification for herself. She submits to her husband, but only to please him; and, but for the desire of maternity, would far rather be relieved from his attentions."

She wants to be relieved from engaging in sexual intercourse because the act was thought to be bestial. As a wife, it was her duty to submit now and then to the beast in her husband's nature. Coition, however, was the undignified, irrational act of animals who allowed themselves to be controlled by the force of powerful emotions. The Victorian woman was dignified, and because she was rational, "Love for her husband and a wish to gratify his passion, and in some women the knowledge that they would be deserted for courtezans if they did not waive their own inclinations, may induce the indifferent, the passionless to admit the embrace of their husbands." Pleasure from sex, enjoyment of intercourse, was out of the question.

Very much to the point was repressing sexual expression. Dr. Acton was specific on this score. The foreskin on a penis, for example, was dangerous because it aroused sexuality: "It affords an additional surface for the excitement of the reflex action, and aggravates an instinct rather than supplies a want. . . . In the unmarried it additionally excites the sexual desires, which it is our object to repress." During waking hours all thoughts of sexual activities had to be successfully repressed or one would pay the penalty for such thoughts at night by having harmful emissions. A person with a pure mind did not think of sex, and he could sleep well at night. The impure, those who thought of libidinous subjects during the day, would have lascivious dreams at night. "A will which in our waking hours we have not exercised in repressing sexual desires, will not, when we fall asleep, preserve us from carrying the sleeping echo of our waking thoughts farther than we dared to do in the daytime." Since Dr. Acton was a knowledgeable physician, in fact a specialist on sexual matters, his beliefs about human sexual behavior must be far more outrageous to us than the beliefs of a layman in the Victorian age.

Professional and lay beliefs coincided on how best to treat children and their mothers when it came to sex education: keep them pure by keeping them ignorant.

> In a state of health no sexual impression should ever affect a child's mind or body. All its vital energy should be employed in building up the growing frame, in storing up external impressions, and educating the brain to receive them. During a well-regulated childhood, and in the case of ordinary temperaments, there is no temptation to infringe this primary law of nature. . . . In healthy subjects, and especially in children brought up in the pure air, and amid the simple amusements of the country, perfect freedom from, and indeed total ignorance of, any sexual affection is, as it should always be, the rule. . . . Thus it happens that with most healthy and well-brought up children, no sexual notion or feeling has ever entered their heads, even in the way of speculation.

Here Dr. Acton dismisses sexual curiosity in children, he ignores involuntary sexual reflex actions, and he forgets that children masturbate. His overriding concern is wanting to believe that children are sexually pure and innocent. The same concern for purity and innocence colors his view of the Victorian matron: "The best mothers, wives, and managers of households, know little or nothing of sexual indulgences. Love of home, children, and domestic duties, are the only passions they feel." This lady was the perfect ideal of an English wife and mother.

The Victorians wanted desperately to believe that their wives and mothers were sexually pure and so they placed women on a towering pedestal the better to idolize them; on the pedestal, women served as constant reminders that society wanted them isolated. From this height Mother could also deliver moral caveats to her children: "Son, do not disgrace me by being sexually mischievous; daughter, do not imperil your chances of someday standing where I stand" Thus, the Victorian woman became a living embodiment of sexual sanctions. She was perhaps more alienated from her own sexuality than any man because she had a constant role to play as moral guardian of her society, her relations, and her home. She stabilized the Victorian family, which was the single most important unit in preserving the order of nineteenth century England. To help support her in a difficult and important role, society exaggerated her virtues and developed codes of behavior to protect those virtues. The aggregate of those codes defines Victorian prudery.

In *The Victorian Frame of Mind,* Walter E. Houghton suggested that prudery was inevitable in the decades from 1830 to 1870: "The pretension to excessive piety and virtue often took a particular form peculiar to the period. When a new middle class, determined to be proper, was too unsure of itself to risk anything that might be thought vulgar, and when Evangelicalism and the fear of sensuality encouraged a rigid censorship, the affectation of prudery was certain to occur."[12] The studied display of virtue which often became absurd because of its excess was inclusive of an affected diction to avoid all suggestions of sexual meaning, the wearing of prodigious amounts of clothing to conceal the body, expurgating the classics in the manner of Thomas Bowdler's treatment of Shakespeare, exhibiting shock at off-color remarks, restraining the delivery and response to humorous conversation, and deliberately ignoring the existence of sexual activities in human life. Most of this, Houghton would say, "was simply an excessive censorship intended to protect and support the code of chastity, or to prevent the embarrassment of looking at what was felt to be shameful."[13] Victorian prudery was actually a manifestation of society's obsession with denying its own sexuality.

This denial was frequently extended to matters of health and hygiene. A respectable woman, married or single, was examined in a doctor's office with a chaperone present. She did not talk about unmentionable parts of her body, and neither did the doctor. If he had to probe for a localized area of pain, he did so through the woman's clothing since she would not get undressed. Some physicians put dummies in their consulting rooms and the patient would point out troublesome areas on the dummy. Even babies were sometimes delivered by doctors or midwives who had to grope for the child under bedclothes. And when it came to personal hygiene, a respectable woman refused to acknowledge her private parts. She took cold baths to sublimate sexual desires (so did her husband and children), but washing the genitals, especially for the male, might evoke impure thoughts, or worse, lead to masturbation. Victorian prudery had its own code of behavior for the family bathroom; it made little allowance for sexual hygiene.

A code of respectable behavior for the seaside prohibited mixed bathing. Women had to remain on one side of a beach sectioned off by nets, bathing boxes, or fences; men stayed on the other side. The well-to-do Englishman who wanted to bathe with his family did so by evading Mrs. Grundy at the Isle of Wight or at resorts on the northern coast of France.

In France, one did not have to be so on guard when speaking. At table a fowl might still have a bosom rather than a breast, and though a rump roast would have been an unmentionable piece of meat, the limbs of chairs and women were legs, and human ankles were once again recognized parts of the anatomy. In England, euphemisms were plentiful. A baby was not "naked"; he was "in birthday attire." The word "belly" gave way to "stomach," which was itself too strong for the publisher of Anthony Trollope's *Barchester Towers* (1857); he changed "fat stomach" to "deep chest." Undergarments became "unmentionables," "sit-down-upons," or "indispensables."

Prudery was responsible for visual as well as oral censorship. Piano legs and bed legs were covered with frills so that people would not think of the nether parts of the anatomy. On a valentine card, Cupid wore a skirt, but he was still relatively undressed compared to the Victorian woman. She wore drawers and ankle-length pantalettes that were frilled, embroidered, scalloped, and always opaque. With the unaccountable exception of evening clothes, where the top of a woman's breasts might show, female attire encased the figure from head to foot. Yards of material proclaimed that the woman was unapproachable. Her dress and her diction let the world know that she was sexually pure; she was respectable.

The most respectable lady of the nineteenth century, the very model of virtue, dignity and propriety, was Queen Victoria herself. From 1821 she had been trained and educated in seclusion to succeed her uncle to the throne. When William IV died on June 20, 1837, Victoria was prepared to do her duty, and to be good. In 1840 she married her cousin Albert and in seventeen years gave the Prince Consort nine children. Her loyalty to Albert and her happy family life were well publicized and politically effective in assuring the country that the Queen was strong of character, morally firm, and unimpeachably virtuous. Victoria was earnest, dedicated, sober, and prudish. If she was not amused by a suggestive story, her displeasure spoke for the age. No less approved than her taste for genteel conversation was her cultural taste. Martin Tupper was one of Victoria's favorite poets, and on the strength of her patronage the *Proverbial Philosophy* went through fifty editions. In art, the Queen and her husband liked what the age liked, or what the age demanded. Here, too, Victorian taste was befitting the well-bred family.

Moral content was of primary importance to viewers of Victorian art. It was looked for, and praised when found, by reviewers for journals such as the *Christian Remembrancer, The Athenaeum, The Times,* and *Fraser's Magazine*. The popular painting was didactic: it taught religious values, it taught social lessons, it told an edifying story. Whether a message was social propaganda or religious instruction, the Victorian painter who won polite approval for his work virtually put a sermon on canvas. The sermon was frequently laced with strong dashes of sentimentality, and this only helped an Augustus Leopold Egg, or William Frederick Yeames or Sir Edwin Landseer. They gave the public scenes of repentant sinners, mournful dogs lying near a master's grave, and young women in states of religious beatitude. In short, they, too, responded to the wants of Victorian respectability.

And no wonder. The pressures to conform were enormous. If social sanctions indicate a society's fear of something, then the Victorian age was terrified of sexual expression. With all of the formal apparatus, the institutional apparatus, working to maintain everyday obedience to the conventions of society, there was in addition the discipline imposed by individuals themselves. This discipline was of an incalculable effect.

Any given employer was likely to fire an unconventional employee. No suitor could win the hand of his lady in accepted fashion before he passed examination by immediate family and relatives. Business life and social life had the quality of propriety, a propriety which was individually upheld by self-discipline, self-denial, and self-restraint. In country and city there were extralegal ways of enforcing the good life. From birth to death for the average Victorian the observance of respectability was not a way of life but *the* way of life. He was born into a prudish family that taught conformity, valued his chastity, and encouraged the homely virtues. He found these values rewarded in school, at work, and by the people with whom he associated. His church and his government, his laws and his betters made sure he would be a proper Victorian.

This life was reflected in early and mid-nineteenth-century literature, and the literature in turn helped to stabilize and perpetuate that very way of life. There is ample scholarly testimony to the effect that writers of quality literature were significantly influenced by the moral forces of their age. To Steven Marcus, "There is no doubt that the Victorian conventions of censorship had a severely limiting effect on the range of the novel."[14] Jerome Buckley used similar language to make the same observation: "Literary reticence concerning matters of sex placed some real limitation upon the content of the novel." Buckley explained, "To the new 'puritans,' who constituted the core of a widened reading public, sexual license and unwed passion meant a permanent threat to the stability of the home, and the home itself seemed the essential fixed unit in an ordered community." Walter Houghton noted that the Victorians tried to control sexual passion by concealment and censorship: "The effort was natural enough at a time when so white a purity was demanded that only extreme measures seemed capable of preserving it from taint or corruption." Richard D. Altick concluded that by the mid-third of the century novelists had bowed to pressure, and he put the matter in practical terms: "To find a market in the purified society of Victorian days they had to conform to rigid moral specifications." Victorian literature was written in an era that demanded and rewarded purity, wholesomeness, and virtue. The sexually pure society wanted sexually pure novels and poems to construct an unimpeachable image of itself. This image was meant to reassure the Victorians of their own righteousness and to preserve their public character for posterity.

II

For the vast majority of Victorians their public character was the same as it was in private. Their sexual morality in public life was no different from their sexual morality in private life. A minority of both men and women compromised their standards and were occasionally promiscuous, read French novels or pornographic literature, now and then frequented underworld haunts, and, in moments, gave in to the age-old sins that flesh seems heir to. A still smaller group thrived on sexual immorality; these were the pornographers and their publishers, kept women and adulterous men, prostitutes and their pimps, sexual deviates and underworld characters with varied interests. Accurate statistics to help measure each and every aspect of Victorian society are impossible to get, but there was certainly an active, energetic life going on that defied the bans established by the official, public morality.

This side of Victorian life has been slighted by scholars; worse, it has been exploited and misrepresented by some who have given it attention. Leo Markun's *Mrs. Grundy* (1930) is a case in point. Crane Brinton said of the book, "For the cheap criticism of the Victorians as prudes, sex-starved and repressed but scandal loving, see Leo Markun,

Mrs. Grundy."[15] The contribution by Cyril Pearl, *The Girl with the Swansdown Seat* (1956), lives up to the notices on its pocket-book cover: "A witty, audacious view of the respectable Victorians, whose virtue was exceeded only by their vices." Beneath the bold letters, PASSIONATE PRUDES, are these lines: "Here is an eye-opening tour of the gaudy, bawdy world that flourished beneath the self-righteously proper façade of Victorian England—that wild and raucous place where fashionable harlots rode with duchesses in Rotten Row, while diplomats and gentry openly negotiated for their favors . . . and sometimes even married them." The one recent book of a different stripe on the sexual subculture of the nineteenth century is Steven Marcus' *The Other Victorians* (1966). In a review of this work, Mark Spilka said, "His [Marcus'] methods offer light in an underworld where scholars seldom tread, and where the usual trashy exposé (for instance, Cyril Pearl's *The Girl with the Swansdown Seat*) only darkens darkness."[16]

The core of Marcus' book is an analysis of seven pornographic novels. Nearly half of his book, one hundred and twenty pages, is devoted to *My Secret Life,* an eleven-volume, anonymously published history of sexual escapades and fantasies written by an upper-middle-class mid-Victorian. Only three sets of the volumes now exist, but because of an abundance of quotations, and because of his evident critical acumen, one has little trouble accepting Marcus' estimate of the work:

> *My Secret Life* shows us that amid and underneath the world of Victorian England as we know it—and as it tended to represent itself to itself—a real, secret social life was being conducted, the secret life of sexuality. Every day, everywhere, people were meeting, encountering one another, coming together, and moving on. And although it is true that the

> Victorians could not help but know of this, almost no one was reporting on it; the social history of their own sexual experiences was not part of the Victorian's official consciousness of themselves or of their society.[17]

Pornography contributes to the social history of sexual experience when one remains aware of the fact that pornography often confuses reality and fantasy. There is enough additional evidence of the nineteenth-century subculture, however, to validate a partial reading of pornography as social history.

Walter Houghton, for example, studied Victorian society from a socio-historic point of view and concluded that the major reason why sex was so frightening to the Victorians was that "sexual license in England not only existed on a large scale but seemed to be increasing."[18] Houghton found sixteen books and twenty-six articles on prostitution published in England and Scotland between 1840 and 1870. One of the articles, which appeared in the *Westminster Review* for 1850, estimated that fifty thousand prostitutes were known to the police in England and Scotland at mid-century. Eight thousand of the women were in London. These figures lack census accuracy, and so do all figures on the subject from any source, but they establish both the reality of prostitution in England and, when taken with other estimates, the vague idea people have and had as to its extent. Richard Lewinsohn in the book quoted earlier, said,

> At the beginning of Queen Victoria's reign police statistics gave only 7,000 prostitutes in London, a moderate number for a city with a population of 2,000,000. Unofficial estimates, it is true, put the figure much higher and the Chief of Police himself admitted the existence of 933 brothels and 848 houses of questionable reputation, which suggests that his own figure for prostitutes was too low, for London always had a large number of street-walkers.[19]

In 1857, Dr. William Acton also guessed at figures in his medical treatise on prostitution: he noted that forty-two thousand illegitimate children were born in England and Wales in 1851 and on that basis estimated, "one in twelve of the unmarried females in the country above the age of puberty have strayed from the path of virtue."[20] Here again one confronts the confusion of reality and fantasy.

On the Continent, prostitution was public, regulated, and licensed; in England, it was private and neither regulated nor licensed. Thus, accurate, official statistics are not available. Ignoring numbers altogether, Sir Philip Magnus makes the safest kind of guess: "During the nineteenth century the number of street-walking prostitutes in London, and other big cities, was much greater than it is today; and the subject was then veiled under a heavy taboo."[21] Despite the taboo, streetwalking was widespread, and widely known about. W. E. Gladstone made the rescuing of prostitutes his principal social and charitable work. He helped to found the Church Penitentiary Association for the Reclamation of Fallen Women (1848), the Clewer Home of Mercy (1854), the Newport Home of Refuge (1863), and the St. Mary Magdalen Home of Refuge (1865). Gladstone personally looked for women to help by going through London streets at night; he would wait to be accosted by a prostitute, or would himself accost her, and then try to persuade her to reform her life. Another public figure who did this kind of thing was Charles Dickens. From 1847 to 1858 Dickens was chairman of an administrative committee which ran a reformatory home for prostitutes, a home which Dickens helped to found. Such homes never appear in a Dickens novel.

Whereas Dickens in print was reticent about prostitution, Fyodor Dostoevsky dealt with the subject explicitly in *Winter Notes on Summer Impressions,* a collection of articles which contain Dostoevsky's impressions of London gathered during a visit from July 9 to July 17, 1862. He writes as a tourist:

> Anyone who has ever visited London has probably been to the Haymarket, if only once. This is the quarter which at night is crowded with women of the street. The streets are lighted by clusters of gas jets of which we have no idea in our country. Magnificent coffee-houses, ornamented with mirrors of gold, at every step. There are crowds of people here. . . . There is no room for the crowds on the pavements and they spill over into the roadway. All of them are intent on some booty and rush with shameless cynicism upon the first man who crosses their path. There the ragged and the resplendent, the extremes of youth and age—all jostle together. In this terrible crowd you will find a drunken tramp and a rich man of title. You hear curses, quarrels, touting, and the gentle, inviting whisper of a still timid pretty girl. And what beauties you sometimes come across![22]

The description of this scene tells more than police estimates of London streetwalkers. It tells that people were indeed openly encountering one another, coming together, and moving on. Further, Dostoevsky testifies to outright solicitation: "In the Haymarket I saw mothers who had brought their young daughters, girls still in their teens, to be sold to men. Little girls of about twelve seize you by the hand and ask you to go with them." An incident such as this appears in a tourist's notebook, or, with great elaboration, in a pornographic novel; it does not appear in quality literature, for here the Victorian deals with a public product for public consumption, and perverse sexual incidents are hidden.

Society's agreement to hide sexuality probably explains why there were laws against prostitution, which was punishable as an act of public scandal, and why there were no laws against procurers. A prostitute had to sell herself by means of highly visual advertisements; she forced herself into the public mind, and that mind was made uneasy. Panders or pimps, on the other hand, communicated orally. They could work in private and remain unseen. Since the public was not forced to recognize them, the law did not recognize them; in fact, throughout the early and mid-Victorian age there was no penalty at all attached to the inducement to prostitution, nor was procuring an indictable offense. A girl was safer in a brothel than on the street, although certain brothels did call themselves to public attention and then were raided. There were houses which catered to flagellants, masochists, and homosexuals. Practices that went on here were too extreme to let pass.

The same kind of agreement which applied to sexual behavior also in a way applied to sexual literature. The French novels of Honoré de Balzac, Eugène Sue, and George Sand were not part of the official consciousness of society, they were not on the recommended reading lists of publicly respectable people, and yet they were privately being read while outwardly being denounced as the literature of prostitution. A private practice was tolerated if it did not pretend to have public acceptance, did not call attention to itself too loudly, and was not too extreme. On the borderline of provoking public outrage were a number of cheap papers that sold from the middle thirties into the sixties, papers such as *Peeping Tom, Paul Pry,* the *Fast Man,* the *Town,* the *Fly,* the *Star of Venus,* and the *London Satirist.* Crossing the line was outright pornographic literature.

Like prostitution, pornography was forbidden by authority, and widespread in practice. From mid-century on, production and sales combined to make it a thriving industry. Its popularity in no small part must have been due to individual desire to taste socially forbidden fruit. Lying with a prostitute or reading pornography was less an infraction of moral law than getting away with something under social and legal conventions which were simply too rigid for wholesome compliance. Breaking the convention seemed to harm no one, and it could be done in private. Furthermore, pornography held the lure of freedom and license; it meant release in fantasy from the sexual restraints of reality. As Steven Marcus discovered,

> For every warning against masturbation issued by the official voice of culture, another work of pornography was published; for every cautionary statement against the harmful effects of sexual excess uttered by medical men, pornography represented copulation *in excelsis,* endless orgies, infinite daisy chains of inexhaustibility; for every assertion about the delicacy and frigidity of respectable women made by the official culture, pornography represented legions of maenads, universes of palpitating females; for every effort made by the official culture to minimize the importance of sexuality, pornography cried out—or whispered—that it was the only thing in the world of any importance at all.[23]

Perhaps a more significant way of putting that last thought would be to say that pornography cried out in silence. Reading is a private act done in communion only with oneself and a speechless page. A brothel devoted to flagellation was much more likely to be exposed than a man sitting alone in his living room reading about flagellation. Pornography allowed one to break taboos he wanted to break in secret. At the same time, any reader might vocally join in public outrage against a visible publication, while knowing he is an invisible reader.

If the Victorians broke sexual taboos by reading pornography, some of them also defied the taboos more actively in their everyday lives. Little is known about the average man who failed to abide by the proprieties of married life, but biographers have provided information about nineteenth-century literary figures. The information does not shock anyone today, and yet it often alters the image of a closely knit family bound by many children and loving ties between husband and wife who are sexually restrained, wholly devoted, and absolutely pure of mind.

Thomas Carlyle and Jane Baillie Welsh had a troublesome marriage, no children, and each made the other sexually uneasy. Carlyle may have been wholly or partially impotent, but he estranged his wife by his fervent admiration of Lady Harriet Baring, later Lady Ashburton. Jane was a coquette who flirted with men before and after her marriage. One of the Carlyles' friends, John Stuart Mill, fell in love with a married woman when he was in his mid-twenties. He and Mrs. Harriet Taylor had an intimate friendship, with Mr. Taylor's knowledge, for nearly twenty years before Mrs. Taylor was free to marry. Charlotte Brontë was passionately drawn to a married man, the Belgian professor Constantin Héger. William Makepeace Thackeray also found himself involved in marital difficulties. After his wife, Isabella Shawe, was committed to an asylum for the insane in 1842, he fell deeply in love with Mrs. William Brookfield, the wife of a close Cambridge friend. In 1851 Mr. Brookfield told his wife to see less of Thackeray.

One of the better-known lives in the nineteenth century is Charles Dickens'. After fathering ten children, Dickens was legally separated from Catherine Hogarth in May, 1858. A precipitating cause of the separation was the fact that Dickens, when he was forty-five years old, fell in love with the actress Ellen Ternan, who was then eighteen. Although their attachment seems to have been sexually innocent for a while, there is little doubt that Ellen soon became Dickens' mistress.

Another prominent Victorian who kept a mistress was the publisher John Chapman. While Chapman lived in London at number 142 on the Strand, he supported at that address his wife, Susanna, and his companion, Elizabeth Tilley. In 1850, he courted a lodger he had accepted named Marian Evans, who was soon to become the novelist George Eliot. Before beginning her novels, however, she began her famous liaison with George Henry Lewes.

Lewes had a reputation for being promiscuous before he became devoted to George Eliot as her common-law husband. At the age of twenty-five, he and his first wife lived a communal life in a house which contained five married couples and two unmarried sisters. Lewes' wife had two children by his best friend, Thornton Hunt. Since he had once condoned his wife's association with Hunt, since he himself was promiscuous, and since divorce, which was only granted by an act of Parliament, was very expensive, Lewes was never legally free to marry George Eliot. They lived together, however, for twenty-four years. When George Henry Lewes died in 1878, George Eliot accepted consolation from a family friend, J. W. Cross. Two years later, Cross, who was forty years old, married George Eliot, who was then sixty-one.

Another person who adored George Eliot was Edith Simcox, a journalist, linguist, manufacturer, trades unionist, lecturer, and school inspector. K. A. McKenzie's *Edith Simcox and George Eliot* (1961) clearly shows that Edith's passionate devotion to Eliot was based in large part on a physical attraction. Lesbian feelings are easily identifiable, and McKenzie discusses those feelings with fewer reservations than one finds when reading biographers who deal with Alfred Tennyson's homosexual feelings for Arthur Henry Hallam. Tennyson's homosexuality remains debatable.

The unfortunate story of John Ruskin's perversion has become academically accepted. Ruskin could not consummate his marriage with Effie Gray, and in 1855 she left him to marry his close friend, the painter John Millais.

In later years, Ruskin was drawn to very young girls, an obsession which culminated in his attachment, at the age of forty, to Rose La Touche, who was eleven. Quite as unhappy as Ruskin's marriage was George Meredith's. In 1849, at the age of twenty-one, George Meredith married Mary Ellen Nicolls, a widow seven years his senior and the mother of a three-year-old daughter. In 1858, Mrs. Meredith ran off with a painter, Henry Wallis, who subsequently deserted her. Broken marriages and perversions occur more frequently later in the century, but there is no need to go into them here.

The private lives of some Victorians were obviously not in accord with the public image the majority wished to construct. This does not mean, however, that the well-publicized clichés about Victorian sexual morality are merely a coverup for an era's wholesale sexual license. It does not mean that for every family strictly bound by moral conventions there was some matching family breaking those conventions. Jerome Buckley tried to balance opposing acts and opposing ideas in an attempt to show how the outlines of the age blurred beyond recognition amidst the confusion of contradictory charges: "While they professed 'manliness,' they yielded to feminine standards; if they emancipated woman from age-old bondage, they also robbed her of a vital place in society. Though they were sexually inhibited and even failed to consider the existence of physical love, they begat incredibly large families and flaunted in their verses a morbidly overdeveloped erotic sensibility."[24] But Buckley was seriously taken to task for setting out to prove that the bewildering complexity of the era presented a culture so various, so diverse, that, in Mario Praz's language, "far from presenting a homogeneous bourgeois aspect, self-satisfied, sentimental, and firmly rooted on unshakeable foundations, the Victorian epoch was a period of extreme restlessness, in which nothing was more stable than in the most dynamic period of English history, the Elizabethan."[25]

Mario Praz wrote an essay entitled "The Victorian Mood: A Reappraisal" as a direct, argumentative challenge to Buckley's view that the Victorian temper is elusive and "Victorianism" merely a figment of the imagination. While Buckley showed the variety of Victorian culture, Praz argues that he missed the forest for the trees:

> What matters is the kind of tree that impresses its character on the wood, and a man who maintains that a garden in Europe is a tropical garden because of one or two rickety palm trees growing there would hardly be taken seriously. Professor Buckley's contention is true to the extent that men have always been the same, under Semiramis as well as under Queen Victoria, but is at the same time false when, laying undue stress on a quantity of tendencies destined to a brief life (who, nowadays, remembers the Spasmodic School of poets of the eighteen fifties?), he proceeds to deny the existence of a Victorian temper distinct from that of the preceding and following periods. In a garden, if I may be allowed to pursue the botanical simile, there will always be a variety of flowers, but those command attention which yield the prevailing scent.[25]

The simile is appropriate, for where there are flowers there will be weeds; where there is morality, there will be immorality. The surface of Victorian life was morally attractive; its subsurface was morally different. The morality which impressed its character on the age and on history, however, was not of a sexual subculture, a Victorian underground, but of a dominant culture whose watchwords were those we still associate with the word "Victorian."

Certainly adultery existed in the nineteenth century, but it was the exception, not the rule in married life. Pornography was widespread, and yet its output was negligible compared to the vast quantities of nonsexual and sexually proper literature which was produced. Unmarried virgins outnumbered prostitutes, perverts were decidedly small in number, and sexual improprieties were shocking, not commonplace. Victorian society did not resemble Elizabethan society, just as it does not resemble society today. Though not in mint condition, the stamp of the age was respectability. The stamp was publicly exhibited and, for the most part, privately cherished. Its relative purity even makes it unique for historians of sexual experience in English societies.

To put the age in focus, one has only to recall the forces which exerted moral pressure to forge its sexual character. There was the Church, especially the Low Church Evangelicals and incredibly energetic Methodists. There were prodigious amounts of religious literature, and various laws, including censorship laws, to legislate the purity of other kinds of literature. Reformist societies were on guard, and so were Utilitarians. Schools helped to protect the national character, and so did publishers, editors, and booksellers. There was family upbringing, the restrictive nature of sex education, and the unmeasurable effect of growing up and living in a prudish society headed by a Queen who was a constant reminder of what that society stood for. The social sanctions which operated to preserve sexual respectability were enormous.

This was the essential nature of the society in which quality literature was written. The Victorian writer grew up under these conditions, wrote under these conditions, and, what must not be overlooked, he had to satisfy these conditions in print if he wanted to market his work successfully. Sexual irregularities had to be consciously removed in the revision of a novel or poem, or, what was more likely, they had to be repressed during the initial act of composition. Sexual repression was both a social and an artistic way of life. But whereas repressed sexuality could, when necessary, find a social outlet in the realm of the Victorian subculture, which hid it from view, the artistic manifestations of sexual repression are always visible to a degree in literature. Sexual experience in Victorian literature, experience that had to be repressed in the early and mid-nineteenth century, is apparent to the twentieth-century reader who allows modern psychology to furnish him with a point of view. This reader has an understanding of the dynamics of sexual repression, a subject discussed in the Appendix to this book.

2
The Problem of Intention

Once sexually repressed materials do become apparent to the psychologically informed reader, he must next deal with the vexing problem of authorial intent. When a poem or novel is well explicated and the explication is presented articulately and persuasively, one always has a suspicion that the poet or novelist intended such a reading at the very time he wrote. College students who spend weeks studying a poem for a class will be amazed that an instructor can find meaning they did not find in the poem, and if the instructor shows his reading to be clear and inescapable, the students will feel that the poet surely intended such a reading in the first place. After years of teaching a poem in class after class, undergraduate and graduate, the college professor who reads a convincing essay on the poem in a scholarly journal will wonder how he could have possibly missed so much for so long; in the back of his mind will be the nagging thought that here was meaning the author intended as he wrote his poem.

This concern for an author's intention persists in the minds of educated readers no matter how often they affirm that much literary activity is unconscious, or that writers cannot be aware of all the implications and meanings of their work. In *The Verbal Icon* (1954), W. K. Wimsatt, Jr., made us intellectually aware of the pitfalls of the intentional fallacy, and yet we constantly approach the traps. For an example of how alluring the problem of authorial intent can be, consider the following situation from Henry James's first novel, *Watch and Ward.*

Nora Lambert, aged twelve, is adopted by a young man named Roger, who secretly hopes Nora will marry him when she has reached maturity. After the adoption, Roger wonders about the benefits of premature lovemaking. "The ground might be gently tickled to receive his own sowing; the petals of the young girl's nature, playfully forced apart, would leave the golden heart of the flower but the more accessible to his own vertical rays." The sexual imagery is unmistakable, but was it intentional? Leon Edel points out the passage in *Henry James, The Conquest of London* (1962). Edel says, "This is a curious passage to come from an inveterate reader of French novels. It may have been penned tongue-in-cheek; yet it may represent also a certain unconscious eroticism."[1] Professor Edel seems quite certain of unconscious sexuality on James's part in subsequent lines which concern Nora, Roger, and Hubert Lawrence, who, like Roger, is interested in the girl. Nora comes to them before she goes to bed, bringing her watch to be wound. Roger's key is a "misfit," but Hubert's key works, although "some rather intimate fumbling was needed to adjust it to Nora's diminutive timepiece."

Both of these passages appeared in the serial version of *Watch and Ward* and in the book version which was published eight years later, in 1878. The sexual overtones now so evident were unnoticed by J. T. Fields, the editor of *Atlantic Monthly,* William Dean Howells, his assistant, the typesetters of the *Atlantic,* and Henry's watchful brother, William James. More than once William and William Dean Howells censored shocking or unfelicitous materials in Henry's prose, but neither man, nor Henry himself, saw sexual meaning where Professor Edel has shown it to us.

Literary critics, historians, or biographers rarely have as much evidence as Edel had to guide them to a decision about an individual author's conscious or unconscious intentions. Records and worksheets disappear, authors and their contemporaries pass away. Even with information available to him, Edel can only guess that Henry James was unaware of the overt elements of sexuality he wrote of between Roger and Nora in *Watch and Ward*. The final conclusion must be, "How conscious he [Henry James] was of this is a moot point."[2] A psychologically oriented critic will agree with this conclusion and still feel a writer such as Henry James would only publish sexually shocking passages were he unaware of their content. A critic who discounts the psychological approach to literature will agree with the conclusion and feel that sex, if it is present in James, was meant to be present. To a critic of this kind, an artist such as James would know what he was about; Freudians are notorious for reading sex into everything, for seeing sex everywhere; and they have underhand ways of interpreting literature.

The better, more truthful word for "underhand" is invalid, and when Freudian analysis is misused, it can definitely lead to invalid criticism. Three conditions will often prepare people to accept a sexual reading of literature: first, a particular passage needs to be isolated; second, a reader must be made to think about sex; third, the critic must talk seriously and confidently about his subject. These three steps can be taken in any order and they need not involve lengthy discussion. For example, consider the following paragraphs on George MacDonald's novel, *Wilfrid Cumbermede* (1872).

Wilfrid, an orphan, has discovered a mechanical toy in a lumber room. As the child plays with his toy, there are clear indications that his play is combined with the serious business of masturbation. To begin with, Wilfrid's attention is focused solely on one part of the toy:

> It had a kind of pendulum . . . my fancy concerning it was that if I could keep the pendulum wagging long enough, it would set [the] trees [outside the window] going too; and if

> I still kept it swinging, we should have such a storm of wind as no living man had ever felt or heard of. . . . I had not . . . had the courage to keep up the oscillations beyond ten or a dozen strokes; partly from fear of the trees, partly from a dim dread of exercising power whose source and extent were not within my knowledge. I kept the pendulum in the closet . . . and never spoke to any one of it.

Sometime later, Wilfrid decides,

> I was nearly a man now; I would be afraid of things no more; I would get out my pendulum, and see whether that would not help me. Not this time would I flinch from what consequences might follow . . . I strode to the closet in which the awful instrument dwelt. . . . I set it in motion, and stood watching it. It swung slower and slower. It wanted to stop. It should not stop. I gave it another swing. On it went, at first somewhat distractedly, next more regularly, then with slowly retarding movement. But it should not stop. . . . I sat and watched it with growing awe, but growing determination as well. Once more it showed signs of refusal; once more the forefinger of my right hand administered impulse. Something gave a crack inside the creature: away went the pendulum swinging with a will. I sat and gazed almost horror-stricken. Ere many moments had passed, the feeling of terror had risen to such a height that, for the very terror, I would have seized the pendulum in a frantic grasp. I did not.

Finally, Wilfrid decides to take the pendulum to bed with him "and stifle its motions with the bed-clothes."

This scene was isolated for comment by Robert L. Wolff in a study of George McDonald's fiction entitled *The Golden Key* (1961). Professor Wolff asks, "Can we doubt that we have been reading a description of masturbation?"[3] Obviously, the question is put for effect, since there can be only one answer. The isolated passages unquestionably describe masturbation. But has Wolff tricked us into such a reading, or is the reading truly valid?

Taken in the context of the novel *Wilfrid Cumbermede,* and in the context of its study in *The Golden Key,* the reading is indeed valid. Professor Wolff shows how the novel itself suggests his interpretation, how preceding and subsequent passages prove him to be right, and how his specific analysis of this one episode fits smoothly into his general analysis of the entire novel. And yet the Freudian reading which seems so evident, which seems, in fact, to argue that MacDonald knew what he was writing all along, was first noted in print by Robert Wolff in 1961, just as Leon Edel's reading of *Watch and Ward* was first noted in 1962. The MacDonald and James novels were both before the public nearly ninety years before someone pointed out their sexual elements clearly enough to make one wonder if sex were intentionally present after all.

It is, of course, not only impossible for readers to know the intentions of most, if not all, writers, but an author himself may think he is writing one thing while he is in fact writing something quite different. Even when he accomplishes in print what he sets out to do, there are overtones, connotations, and meanings to his work which may escape him. Furthermore, the elusive significance we call "meaning" can itself change with time. Neither language nor learning remains constant over the years, and thus "meaning" will be affected by both words and concepts as they turn obsolete or become newly available. Seventeenth-century usage of the verb "to die" as a synonym for sexual intercourse will suggest meaning in certain contexts just as meaning will be found under other circumstances which relate to twentieth-century concepts of depth psychology. The Oedipal complex in *Hamlet* has become so established in our time that people joke about Shakespeare's writing the play with an assist by Sigmund Freud.

The findings of depth psychology, however, generally have a negative bearing on discussions of the intentional fallacy. Most of the obstacles to discovering an author's intentions mentioned in the preceding paragraph have to do with a reader trying to determine what a novelist or poet actually did set out to do as he wrote. Freudian criticism, on the other hand, frequently evokes the response, "Surely Browning or Tennyson, Eliot or Dickens, did *not* intend to write about intercourse, let alone masturbation, incest, homosexuality or lesbianism." One can be convinced that a given author would never consider writing about a particular subject. When such a conviction is ardently held, then the intentional fallacy will operate as the strongest of mental blocks to perception. Those who insist upon prejudging literature will agree with criticism that strengthens their belief about what an author intended to write; they will disagree with criticism that weakens their belief. It is awesome to stand before mystics who know an author's unconscious intentions nearly as well as they know his conscious intentions.

These dyspeptic caveats about intention do not preclude a reader's interest in an author's biography, social condition, or historical presence. The more knowledge we have of the context of art, the better we can appreciate the text of art. In fact, the present study contends that a poem or novel becomes more meaningful when read with an awareness of its psychological prerequisites. And yet there is a difference between knowing about a work of art and knowing the work of art. A particular interpretation of some poem may be harder or easier to believe because of outside, contextual information, but such circumstantial knowledge should never displace the poem itself. Psychology or biography can be of invaluable aid in showing a critic how to look at literature, but the meaning of literature must be internally generated by that literature. Unfortunately, the history of criticism has shown literary meaning to be as elusive as philosophical truth.

The following essays on Victorian literature deal with

novels and poems which have been read for more than one hundred years.[4] The sexual meaning of this literature has been slighted to the extent that several of these essays discuss sexuality in given works for the first time in print. If the discussions are convincing and critically valid, if all interpretations are persuasively shown to have textual support, then some readers may feel that the Victorians were indeed aware of the sexual components of their art, while others may feel that sexual expression in Victorian literature was a product of psychological pressures working on a writer's unconscious mind. We may speculate forever about an author's conscious or unconscious intentions in a given novel or poem, and yet our speculations will always be conjectures based upon insufficient evidence. But perhaps all readers will be able to agree that whatever the Victorians consciously or unconsciously intended to do, the meaning of Victorian literature is greatly expanded when one pays attention to its sexual dimension.

3

Robert Browning's "The Last Ride Together"

Recent years have seen critics beginning to pay attention to sexuality in Robert Browning's poetry. In 1964, William Cadbury published an article in the *University of Toronto Quarterly* wherein he commented on the following stanza from Browning's "Love Among the Ruins":

> Now,—the single little turret that remains
>   On the plains,
> By the caper overrooted, by the gourd
>   Overscored,
> While the patching houseleek's head of blossom winks
>   Through the chinks—
> Marks the basement whence a tower in ancient time
>   Sprang sublime,
> And a burning ring, all round, the chariots traced
>   As they raced,
> And the monarch and his minions and his dames
>   Viewed the games.

The imagery of a tower with a burning ring around its base gave Cadbury the occasion to say, "This phallically dominating and vaginally ringed tower has shrunk to a turret which was in the past only a basement, and even that turret is overgrown by the fertile land."[1] Time has wasted sexual potency, which the poem had signified by a penial erection rooted in pubic hair.

Karl Kroeber gave an unusual reading to the popular "Meeting at Night" in a *Victorian Poetry* issue of Spring, 1965.

Meeting at Night

I

The gray sea and the long black land;
And the yellow half-moon large and low;
And the startled little waves that leap
In fiery ringlets from their sleep,
As I gain the cove with pushing prow,
And quench its speed i' the slushy sand.

II

Then a mile of warm sea-scented beach;
Three fields to cross till a farm appears;
A tap at the pane, the quick sharp scratch
And blue spurt of a lighted match,
And a voice less loud, thro' its joys and fears,
Than the two hearts beating each to each!

Karl Kroeber wrote, "Possibly one has to be steeped in Freudianism at once to recognize the full significance of 'gaining the cove with pushing prow,' but by the closing 'two hearts beating each to each' only a prudish reader will deny that the poem includes a dramatization of the gratifications of physical love." After demonstrating support for his thesis, Kroeber concludes, " 'Meeting at Night' develops a vigorous sub-articulate sensuality."[2]

Better known to the academic community as a Browning scholar than either Cadbury or Kroeber is Robert Langbaum. Taking a broad look at the Victorian poet in a 1966 *PMLA* article, "Browning and the Question of Myth," Langbaum observes,

> We know that Browning's imagination was dominated, throughout his career, by the image of the beautiful Andromeda, chained naked to the rock, waiting helplessly for the serpent to come out of the sea to devour her, but waiting also—though she does not consciously know this—for Perseus to descend miraculously—to "come," as Browning puts it in *Pauline,* "in thunder from the stars"—to rescue her. The

combination of sexual and spiritual ramifications gives the image its strength and validity.[3]

In time, there will be an increasing number of studies which point out sexual and spiritual ramifications to Browning's poetry. This essay on "The Last Ride Together" is one such study.

The Last Ride Together

I

I said—Then, dearest, since 'tis so,
Since now at length my fate I know,
Since nothing all my love avails,
Since all, my life seemed meant for, fails,
Since this was written and needs must be—
My whole heart rises up to bless
Your name in pride and thankfulness!
Take back the hope you gave,—I claim
Only a memory of the same,
—And this beside, if you will not blame,
Your leave for one more last ride with me.

II

My mistress bent that brow of hers;
Those deep dark eyes where pride demurs
When pity would be softening through,
Fixed me a breathing-while or two
With life or death in the balance: right!
The blood replenished me again;
My last thought was at least not vain:
I and my mistress, side by side
Shall be together, breathe and ride,
So, one day more am I deified.
Who knows but the world may end to-night?

III

Hush! if you saw some western cloud
All billowy-bosomed, over-bowed
By many benedictions—sun's
And moon's and evening-stars' at once—

And so, you, looking and loving best,
Conscious grew, your passion drew
Cloud, sunset, moonrise, star-shine too,
Down on you, near and yet more near,
Till flesh must fade for heaven was here!—
Thus leant she and lingered—joy and fear!
Thus lay she a moment on my breast.

IV

Then we began to ride. My soul
Smoothed itself out, a long-cramped scroll
Freshening and fluttering in the wind.
Past hopes already lay behind.
What need to strive with a life awry?
Had I said that, had I done this,
So might I gain, so might I miss.
Might she have loved me? just as well
She might have hated, who can tell!
Where had I been now if the worst befell?
And here we are riding, she and I.

V

Fail I alone, in words and deeds?
Why, all men strive and who succeeds?
We rode; it seemed my spirit flew,
Saw other regions, cities new,
As the world rushed by on either side.
I thought,—All labor, yet no less
Bear up beneath their unsuccess.
Look at the end of work, contrast
The petty done, the undone vast,
This present of theirs with the hopeful past!
I hoped she would love me; here we ride.

VI

What hand and brain went ever paired?
What heart alike conceived and dared?
What act proved all its thought had been?
What will but felt the fleshly screen?
We ride and I see her bosom heave.
There's many a crown for who can reach.
Ten lines, a statesman's life in each!

The flag stuck on a heap of bones,
A soldier's doing! what atones?
They scratch his name on the Abbey stones.
My riding is better, by their leave.

VII

What does it all mean, poet? Well,
Your brains beat into rhythm, you tell
What we felt only; you expressed
You hold things beautiful the best,
And pace them in rhyme so, side by side.
'Tis something, nay 'tis much: but then,
Have you yourself what's best for men?
Are you—poor, sick, old ere your time—
Nearer one whit your own sublime
Than we who never have turned a rhyme?
Sing, riding's a joy! For me, I ride.

VIII

And you, great sculptor—so, you gave
A score of years to Art, her slave,
And that's your Venus, whence we turn
To yonder girl that fords the burn!
You acquiesce, and shall I repine?
What, man of music, you grown gray
With notes and nothing else to say,
Is this your sole praise from a friend,
"Greatly his opera's strains intend,
But in music we know how fashions end!"
I gave my youth; but we ride, in fine.

IX

Who knows what's fit for us? Had fate
Proposed bliss here should sublimate
My being—had I signed the bond—
Still one must lead some life beyond,
Have a bliss to die with, dim-descried.
This foot once planted on the goal,
This glory-garland round my soul,
Could I descry such? Try and test!
I sink back shuddering from the quest.
Earth being so good, would Heaven seem best?
Now, Heaven and she are beyond this ride.

X

And yet—she has not spoke so long!
What if heaven be that, fair and strong
At life's best, with our eyes upturned
Whither life's flower is first discerned,
    We, fixed so, ever should so abide?
What if we still ride on, we two
With life for ever old yet new,
Changed not in kind but in degree,
The instant made eternity,—
And heaven just prove that I and she
    Ride, ride together, forever ride?

In 1915 William Lyon Phelps wrote that Robert Browning's "The Last Ride Together" was "one of the greatest love-poems in all literature."[4] Yale's Lampson Professor of English may have been somewhat too enthusiastic, but through the years his voice has been merely one of a chorus of the poem's admirers: in 1897 Edward Berdoe noted, "This poem is considered by many critics to be the noblest of all Browning's love poems."[5] Arthur Symons wrote in 1906, " 'The Last Ride Together' is one of those love-poems which I have spoken of as specially noble and unique, and it is, I think, the noblest and most truly unique of them all." Almost jealous of its many readers, and perhaps unknowingly defensive, in 1956 Henry C. Duffin said, "No amount of analysis can rob this poem of the deservedly high place it holds with Browning devotees." The poem has had a good deal of analysis from both early and recent critics, and their admiration cannot be robbed of its fervor.[6] However, devotees of this Victorian masterpiece are presently asked to entertain a new understanding of "The Last Ride Together." This understanding draws upon the now vulgar coitional meaning of the word "ride" in order to suggest that the title of Browning's poem is a metaphor which relates significantly to the sexual act.

With the exception of Albert Mordell, no one in print

understands the poem this way. Mordell has a paragraph on "The Last Ride Together" in *The Erotic Motive in Literature,* a book originally published in 1919. The paragraph calls attention to the sexual sense of "to ride," and thus anticipates the direction of my essay by nearly fifty years.[7]

Traditionally, the first stanza of Browning's poem is read as a rejected lover's plea to his lady for their last time together to be spent horseback riding. The lady thinks about this for a "breathing-while" in stanza two, and then agrees. The next two stanzas prepare for and begin the ride. Now the speaker thinks about failure and success as he rides and sees his companion's bosom heave. Stanzas seven and eight declare that the artist—the poet, sculptor, musician—deals less with life than men such as the speaker who personally experience exhilarating moments as they really happen. The poet may sing about the joy of riding, but the speaker actually rides. He is depressed in stanza nine, for his earthly ride has been so enjoyable that he wonders if there could possibly be a more perfect bliss in heaven. "Earth being so good, would heaven seem best?" The last stanza asks if heaven might virtually be "The instant made eternity,"—the climax of the ride prolonged eternally. "And heaven just prove that I and she / Ride, ride together, forever ride?"

Manly resolution characterizes the narrator. Readers have observed that despite immediate failure in courtship, the man is brave and generous. He accepts his situation without any trace of petty vindictiveness; he even blesses the woman for giving him the memory of a past romance. With optimistic cheerfulness, he prepares to relish their last moments together. Browning manages successfully to fuse dramatic intensity and philosophic speculation in a scene that presents both emotional and intellectual involvement. While the narrator rides physically, he mentally ponders the relationship between life and art, and the theory of imperfection which Browning worked on in poems such as "Rabbi Ben Ezra" and "Old Pictures in Florence." But in "The Last Ride Together" there is more, insist Browning enthusiasts. The metrical handling evokes the very breath and blood of equestrian activity. As C. H. Herford has it, "In the wonderful long-drawn rhythm of the verse we hear the steady stride of the horses as they bear their riders farther and farther into the visionary land of Romance."[8]

This poem's rhythmical mastery of riding has sexual overtones that have been long ignored. The *Oxford English Dictionary* records usage from 1250 to 1719 of the verb "to ride" as "To mount the female; to copulate." A variant is recorded to the nineteenth century, from 1500 to 1808: "To mount or cover (the female)." There is no date telling when the word in this sense became used only in low and indecent language. Eric Partridge's *A Dictionary of Slang and Unconventional English* provides an approximate date of 1780 when a definition of "ride" in Standard English was "To mount a woman in copulation." This meaning in colloquial English extends to the twentieth century. Also colloquial in both the nineteenth and twentieth centuries is "ride" as "an act of coition."

George Eliot called attention to Dorothea Brooke's latent sexuality by means of a riding motif in *Middlemarch*: "Most men thought her bewitching when she was on horseback. . . . Riding was an indulgence which she allowed herself in spite of conscientious qualms; she felt that she enjoyed it in a pagan sensuous way" (Ch. I). Eliot also took advantage of the connection between riding and sexuality in *Daniel Deronda.* Gwendolen Harleth is about to go riding with Grandcourt: "She went down in her riding-habit, to avoid delay before getting on horseback. She wanted to have her blood stirred once more with the intoxication of youth" (Book IV). As they ride, Grandcourt declares his love and proposes marriage. "When they had had a glorious gallop, . . . she was in a state of exhilaration that disposed her to think well of hastening the marriage which would make her life all of a piece with this splendid kind of enjoyment." Grandcourt feels triumphant. "She had been brought to accept him in spite of everything—brought to kneel down like a horse under training for the arena." His sexual and physical dominance of Gwendolen is the dominance of a rider over his horse. "Grandcourt inwardly observed that she answered to the rein" (Book V). Late in the novel Eliot says of Grandcourt, "He had the courage and confidence that belong to domination, and he was at that moment feeling perfectly satisfied that he held his wife with bit and bridle" (Book VII).

In an article for the *Victorian Newsletter* (Spring, 1964) entitled, "Sun and Shadow: The Nature of Experience in Tennyson's 'The Lady of Shalott,'" the late Lona Mosk Packer demonstrated Lancelot's sexual attraction for the Lady, and in so doing she might well have joined Lancelot's sexuality and his riding. As Lancelot rides between the barley sheaves, he enters the Lady's sight, "a virility symbol blazing with light." On his shield, "the symbol of sexual dedication, the red-cross knight forever kneeling to his lady." Professor Packer then describes Lancelot:

> He rides in the sun, and he is embellished with all the synonyms for brightness in the poet's formidable word-hoard: the dazzling sun flames upon his brazen leg armour; his shield sparkles; his bridle encrusted with gems glitters like clusters of stars in the golden Galaxy; his helmet and helmet-feather burn like one burning flame; his broad clear brow glows in the sunlight; even the hooves of his war-horse are burnished as he flashes into the crystal mirror.

Lancelot's virility is established by brilliant imagery and

his posture as a rider on horseback. It is this sexual virility which attracts the Lady.

More recent poets than Tennyson have also worked with the sexual connotations of riding. In stanza 28 of "The Wreck of the Deutschland," Gerard Manley Hopkins imagines a nun drawn erotically and spiritually to Christ. "Let him ride, her pride, in his triumph, despatch and have done with his doom there." William Butler Yeats used the word "ride" sexually in a poem entitled "The Three Bushes." A lady who wishes to preserve her chastity has her chambermaid take her place in a lover's bed. The chambermaid and the lover lie between the sheets at midnight each night for all of one year. Stanza seven asks, "Did ever man ride such a race?" And answers, "No, not until he rode."

An outrageously comic use of the word "ride" in the form of a pun on its sexual meaning occurs in Mark Twain's "Letters from the Earth." Satan, writing from Earth to Michael and Gabriel in heaven, describes man's imagined heaven. Satan is astounded that man has left sexual intercourse entirely out of his conception of heaven and replaced this activity with prayer. All men and women prize copulation, but most people dislike prayer. To Satan, it is extraordinary that man would be willing to do without his most prized entertainment.

> I recall to your attention the extraordinary fact with which I began. To wit, that the human being, like the immortals, naturally places sexual intercourse far and away above all other joys—yet he has left it out of his heaven! The very thought of it excites him; opportunity sets him wild; in this state he will risk life, reputation, everything—even his queer heaven itself—to make good that opportunity and ride it to the overwhelming climax.[9]

Satan's outspokenness was certainly not a Victorian characteristic.

To the Victorians, sexual intercourse was not a joking matter. When the colloquial significance of "ride" was recognized in the mid-nineteenth century, the word was immediately censored. Lona Packer tells of such a happening in her critical biography, *Christina Rossetti*. On September 12, 1857, Christina Rossetti wrote part of a poem she called "Nightmare." William Michael first discovered the fragment after his sister's death. When he published the poem, he changed words in the first and last part:

> I have a *love* in ghostland—
> Early found, ah me how early lost!—
> Blood-red seaweeds drip along that coastland
> By the strong sea wrenched and tost . . . .
>
> . . .
>
> If I wake he *rides* me like a nightmare:
> I feel my hair stand up, my body creep:
> Without light I see a blasting sight there,
> See a secret I must keep.

The word "love" became "friend"; the word "rides" became "hunts." Packer observed, "William's substitution in the printed text of two mild and conventional words for the two more psychologically revealing words in manuscript becomes in context a highly significant alteration." In short, William censored the image of intercourse he found in the original stanza.[10]

No passage in Robert Browning's "The Last Ride Together" is quite as sexually explicit as "he rides me." But Packer has helpfully shown where a Victorian poem used an ordinary word in a special sense that was recognized by a Victorian reader. The special sense of "ride" as a semantically vital word with sexual overtones significantly influences my interpretation of "The Last Ride Together."

Browning's poem opens as the speaker recalls being told by his beloved that their intimacy must end. Since "this was written," he accepts his fate, for it "needs must be." His immediate response is to bless the lady's name "in pride and thankfulness," and to request, if she "will not blame," her leave for "one more last ride." His apologetic tone is no less ambiguous than the wording of his request. Does asking a loved one for a final moment's company merit blame? Does asking for one *more* last ride mean that there have been other last rides? Does "last" have the various meanings it has in "My Last Duchess"? The adjective might be simply redundant, or it might be ironic. But if each time the lovers part they go horseback riding, this is indeed too fanciful. If the woman has agreed to intercourse "for the last time," as she might have done several times in the past, then the tone of the proposition is understandable. This reading has the further advantage of providing a smooth transition to stanza two.

The lady, whom the speaker calls "My mistress," bends her brow and fixes the man with "deep dark eyes where pride demurs / When pity would be softening through." She is annoyed, or thoughtfully considering the proposition. While the man waits for her reply "With life or death in the balance," his very blood seems to leave him. Seeing her lover in such emotional distress, would the proud lady object or raise scruples to going horseback riding? Or would pride cause her to reject the expediency of copulation? Pity for the man's emotional condition makes her submit. With "blood replenished" her lover feels "one day more am I deified." The sex act more than any other achievement has "deified" the host of men.

Before the act begins, the man pulls the lady to him, and "thus lay she a moment on my breast." The sensual imagery of stanza three is much more fitting a sexual embrace than the preparations for horseback riding. The speaker asks the reader to imagine a "billowy-bosomed" western cloud blessed by the sun, the moon, the evening-star. As the reader, "looking and loving best," grew conscious of the scene, his passion would draw the night's beauties down on him "near and yet more near, / Till flesh must fade for heaven was here!" Thus does the lady lean and linger in the speaker's embrace, an embrace that has fleshly-spiritual aspects which in part clarify the idea of a physically initiated deification.

When flesh fades, then soul is released, and as the couple begin to ride, the man's soul "Smoothed itself out, a long-cramped scroll / Freshening and fluttering in the wind." In mundane terms, the soul's revitalization may be pictured as occurring when the lady moves from her position on the man's breast to a position more suitable to intercourse and the "ride" begins. One alternative is to imagine the pair, probably dressed in Victorian habits, as they awkwardly hug on horseback and gallop away.

Stanza five suggests that the two do not move physically across the countryside. "It seemed my spirit flew," the speaker says. "Saw other regions, cities new, / As the world rushed by on either side." Key words are "seemed" and "spirit." The man does not literally travel over miles of ground, nor is there any mention here or anywhere else in the entire poem of a journey taken specifically or solely by horse. One reading of the last line in the stanza actually pinpoints a stationary location: "I hoped she would love me; here we ride." Like other men, the speaker had striven for a certain goal, had failed, and now had to "Bear up beneath [his] unsuccess." His hopeful past contrasts with the present: instead of a life-long love, he must be content with a momentary intimacy. The terms of the bargain are consistently amatory.

Thoughts of success and failure now lead the man to extended philosophizing which he punctuates at intervals by returning to his immediate pleasure. Who has ever lived up to his hopes, to his aspirations? Who has ever been able to execute fully what the mind designed? What the heart conceived? Who has never been thwarted by bodily limitations? "We ride and I see her bosom heave." Posterity crowns success with joyless rewards—biographies, memorials, name plates. "My riding is better, by their leave."

Stanzas seven and eight contrast apprehensions of reality. The poet whom the speaker addresses intellectually fashions a meaning to life; the speaker emotionally lives. The poet's "brains beat into rhythm" and "tell / What we felt only." Browning gives us the same argument from a poet's point of view in "Cleon," where the artist writes to a king,

> Indeed, to know is something, and to prove
> How all this beauty might be enjoyed, is more:
> But, knowing naught, to enjoy is something too.
> Yon rower, with the moulded muscles there,
> Lowering the sail, is nearer it that I.
> I can write love-odes: thy fair slave's an ode.
> I get to sing of love, when grown too gray
> For being beloved: she turns to that young man,
> The muscles all a-ripple on his back.
> I know the joy of kingship: Well, thou art king! (ll. 291-300)

The nonartistic speaker of "The Last Ride Together" agrees that the "maker's" life is incomplete. He scores his point with a comparison based upon one of the most telling of human experiences: "Sing, riding's a joy! For me, I ride."

The sculptor deals with lifeless matter. The musician's opera goes out of fashion. Although time takes all things, including the speaker's youth, the artist has less to enjoy of his days than the person caught up in the present, the actual, the physical. A statue pales before its human equivalent and the past gives way to the moment. "We ride, in fine."

Since all men fail, and some can make the most of failure, the speaker has seen himself to be man's equal, or a little more than his equal. He has been confident in his material achievement and in his argument. But as the ride comes to an end in stanza nine, he feels empty and depressed; his previous assurance changes to a questioning hesitancy. The emotional letdown which attends the completion of sexual intercourse might account for the despondent mood. First, he asks, "Who knows what's fit for us?" There is a life after death which should provide one with the highest moments of bliss. This end, though "dim-descried," should surpass the happiness life has to offer. If he approaches this bliss, he wonders, "Could I descry such?" The answer comes quickly: "I sink back shuddering from the quest." What concerns the speaker is literally a matter of religious faith. Celestial promises are suspect if they are prematurely fulfilled in this world. And this is precisely the spiritual problem: "Earth being so good, would heaven seem best?" The good experience which was capable of sublimating his being had to have happened within the course of the poem, for it is this earthly experience which bothers him because of its heavenly perfection. At this point, it seems to be a rhetorical question to ask whether a man's being would be exalted to its highest pitch by the sex act or by horseback riding.

In stanza ten the speaker assures himself that the *summum bonum* is reserved for heaven, that failure or a lesser good is a positive condition of life. He knows that without earthly failure there would be no need for heavenly perfection, and what he had thought was perfection a moment ago merely approached it in degree. He apparently glimpsed heaven at the climax of intercourse; the life beyond would be the emotional feeling infinitely prolonged: "Changed not in kind but in degree, / The instant made eternity." The temporal "instant" can be taken plainly as the moment of sexual bliss, an emotional moment which fulfills both the speaker's secular and religious desires. Earlier he had said, "Flesh must fade for heaven was here." Now the physical and spiritual terms are reversed as the poem ends with the lines, "And heaven prove that I and she / Ride, ride together, forever ride."

The sexual meaning in "The Last Ride Together" complements traditional interpretations: there is still at the heart of the poem the optimistic theory of imperfection, the glory of failure, the notion that the earthly race is better than the earthly prize. A compensatory afterlife rewards mundane defeat; it even increases the value of defeat. Unsuccess in certain moments gives a tantalizing, soul-satisfying vision of heavenly success. Further, faith in real life experience is a religious necessity which points towards spiritual ideals. A concrete example of sexual participation makes this point.

But if for some readers the example is not quite so concrete, not to be taken quite so literally, it still exists in the poem as submerged symbolism. There may be fantasied intercourse in the hero's conscious or semiconscious mind. "The Last Ride Together" does somehow raise the image of copulation to accompany and to evoke a heavenly vision. The image seems perfectly suitable as a fundamental physical achievement in human experience. The poem uses the image to say that fleshly sensation is a concomitant to spiritual deification.

4

Alfred Tennyson's "Lancelot and Elaine" and "Pelleas and Ettarre"

I

Between 1859 and 1885 Tennyson published the poems he was to call his *Idylls of the King*. "Lancelot and Elaine," originally entitled "Elaine," was among the first of the idylls to appear in print, thus making it a harbinger of poems to come. The early poem certainly foreshadowed major themes and events: for example, here is Guinevere's fundamental criticism of King Arthur ("He is all fault who hath no fault at all"), here is her dying love affair with Lancelot, rife with distrust, jealousy, and pettiness, and here, too, one clearly sees the moral disintegration of Arthur's court, especially prominent in the person of Sir Gawain. "Lancelot and Elaine" also points to the sexual preoccupation of the *Idylls,* and it does so in this case by concentrating on the subject of sexual repression. The poem shows how sexual repression can be dynamically portrayed in relation to the psychological phenomenon widely known today as fetishism.

Sigmund Freud told in *Three Essays on the Theory of Sexuality* (1905) how the normal sex object in fetishism is replaced by another object which is entirely unsuited to serve the normal sexual aim. Fetishism usually occurs when the normal sexual aim seems unattainable or its fulfillment prevented; the person concerned frequently makes a symbolic mental association of an available object, which becomes the fetish, with the unavailable sexual object. The substitution of the fetish is made unconsciously, and the person is unaware of having sexual interest in the fetish. But the object become a fetish always has sexual connections with its original. Furthermore, uninvolved observers can easily identify the behavior of a fetishist. Scores of psychologists and psychiatrists have written on the subject of fetishism since Freud, and there is widespread agreement among them. Accepted hypotheses are these: the fetish is overvalued by its owner; it is jealously guarded and the fetishist wants to be its sole possessor; the fetish can displace all other sexual interest; the fetishist derives sexual pleasure from handling the fetish and frequently lavishes sexual attention on the fetish. In *Personality Development and Psychopathology,* Norman Cameron noted, "One of the most widely accepted hypotheses is that the fetish is a substitute for a sex partner, a substitute that makes no demands and is not in itself dangerous."[1] And as a final comment on the theory of fetishism is the observation perhaps immediately evident that a fetish provides an outlet for repressed sexual energy. By means of a fetish, that which is sexually repressed can find innocent sexual expression.

The fetishist in Tennyson's "Lancelot and Elaine" is Elaine; the fetish is Sir Lancelot's shield. Twenty-seven lines which open the poem immediately establish the shield's importance to Elaine:

> Elaine the fair, Elaine the lovable,
> Elaine, the lily maid of Astolat,
> High in her chamber up a tower to the east
> Guarded the sacred shield of Lancelot;
> Which first she placed where morning's earliest ray 5
> Might strike it, and awake her with the gleam;
> Then fearing rust or soilure fashion'd for it
> A case of silk, and braided thereupon
> All the devices blazon'd on the shield

In their own tinct, and added, of her wit, 10
A border fantasy of branch and flower,
And yellow-throated nestling in the nest.
Nor rested thus content, but day by day,
Leaving her household and good father, climb'd
That eastern tower, and entering barr'd her door, 15
Stript off the case, and read the naked shield,
Now guess'd a hidden meaning in his arms,
Now made a pretty history to herself
Of every dint a sword had beaten in it,
And every scratch a lance had made upon it, 20
Conjecturing when and where: this cut is fresh,
That ten years back; this dealt him at Caerlyle,
That at Caerleon—this at Camelot—
And ah, God's mercy, what a stroke was there!
And here a thrust that might have kill'd, but God 25
Broke the strong lance, and roll'd his enemy down,
And saved him: so she lived in fantasy.

Much is made in the idyll of Elaine's living in fantasy (see also ll. 396 and 995), and much more is made of Lancelot's shield. Detailed analysis of the shield as a fetish, however, must await a retelling of the events preceding the situation portrayed in the poem's opening lines. The poem itself is structurally organized by means of a flashback to answer the question, "How came the lily maid by that good shield / of Lancelot, she that knew not even his name?" (ll. 28-29)

The flashback begins with the statement that Lancelot left his shield with Elaine when he rode to tilt in a tournament known as the diamond joust. Then the poem goes far back in time to tell the history of the joust. Once King Arthur found a jeweled crown and decreed there would be a tournament once a year for nine years, with the winner receiving a diamond at the end of each combat. Lancelot had won eight times. Now the last and largest diamond was the prize, a prize Lancelot intended to present along with all of the others he had won to Queen Guinevere.

But Lancelot mistakenly thinks the Queen wants him to stay with her this year instead of jousting, and he lies to the King about a wound which would keep him from the saddle. Guinevere berates him for the act. Lancelot is vexed at having lied in vain, and the two of them plot to have Lancelot enter the tournament disguised as an unknown knight. Since men were said to go down before Lancelot's great name rather than before his spear, King Arthur would appreciate Lancelot's fight for glory as an anonymous combatant.

Thus, Lancelot rides out of Camelot unwilling to be known. He loses his way among solitary downs until he comes upon the Castle of Astolat. The Lord of Astolat, a widower, greets him with two sons, Sir Torre and Sir Lavaine, and with a daughter, the lily maid Elaine. Lancelot asks for and receives a blank shield, and he also gains the company of Lavaine, who would like to enter the diamond joust he has heard about. Lancelot tells him, with reference to Elaine, "And you shall win this diamond,—as I hear / It is a fair large diamond,—if ye may, / And yield it to this maiden, if ye will" (ll. 226-228). The boorish Sir Torre says such diamonds are for queens, not for simple maids, whereupon Sir Lancelot pays Elaine a courtly compliment:

> "If what is fair be but for what is fair,
> And only queens are to be counted so,
> Rash were my judgment then, who deem this maid
> Might wear as fair a jewel as is on earth,
> Not violating the bond of like to like." l. 240

The next 150-odd lines of the poem are devoted to showing how Elaine falls in love with Lancelot.

By the time he has finished speaking, Elaine is "won by the mellow voice before she look'd" (l. 242). To Elaine, "he seem'd the goodliest man / That ever among ladies ate in hall, / And noblest, when she lifted up her eyes" (ll. 253-255). Although Lancelot is more than twice her age, scarred with a sword cut, and marked with the great and guilty love he bore Queen Guinevere, Elaine "lifted up her eyes / And loved him, with that love which was her doom" (ll. 258-259).

Lancelot agrees to dine and stay the night at Astolat. During dinner he tells his hosts stories of the Round Table, including the heroic feats of King Arthur in battle. "I never saw his like; there lives no greater leader" (l. 315). Elaine says to her heart, "Save your great self, fair lord." When Elaine strives to cheer Lancelot from passing fits of melancholy and is rewarded with a sudden-beaming tenderness, "she thought / That all was nature, all, perchance, for her. / And all night long his face before her lived" (ll. 327-329). That night Elaine thinks only of Lancelot. "The face before her lived, / Dark-splendid, speaking in the silence, full / Of noble things, and held her from her sleep" (ll. 335-337).

In the morning, Elaine hears Lancelot cry for his shield.

> There to his proud horse Lancelot turn'd, and smooth'd
> The glossy shoulder, humming to himself.
> Half-envious of the flattering hand, she drew
> Nearer and stood. l. 348

Lancelot is amazed at Elaine's beauty in the morning light; he is also fearful, for "she stood / Rapt on his face as if it were a god's" (l. 354). She asks Lancelot to wear her favor at the tilt, and though he first refuses by saying he never wears favors in the lists, Elaine tells him it will then help to ensure his disguise. He fastens her red sleeve embroidered with pearls to his helmet and tells Elaine he has never before done such a thing for any maiden living. "The blood / Sprang to her face and fill'd her with delight" (l. 375). Then Lancelot asks Elaine to keep his shield until he returns, and he and Lavaine ride off. Elaine stands near the shield in silence while she watches the knights cross the downs. "Then to her tower she climb'd, and took the shield, / There kept it, and so lived in fantasy" (ll. 396).

Meeting Lancelot has been an extraordinary event in Elaine's life. Any sexual experience she had while growing up in the seclusion of Astolat was minimal, for her purity and innocence are stressed throughout the poem, and one cannot doubt that she leads a very sheltered life. She asks,

> "What know I?
> My brethren have been all my fellowship;
> And I, when often they have talk'd of love,
> Wish'd it had been my mother, for they talk'd,
> Meseem'd, of what they knew not." l. 671

One of her brothers, Sir Torre, is an ungracious boor, and her other brother, Sir Lavaine, is an untried youth. Her father dotes upon her and protects her. But Lancelot, even incognito, is a man such as she has never met before. He pays her courtly compliments and entrances her with tales of Camelot and King Arthur's wars. He has the grace and assurance which come from being tried in combat, tried in love, and tried at court. As a woman, the innocent Elaine is overwhelmed by Lancelot's sophistication and experience. And though he rode away without encouraging her love for him, Elaine "ever kept / The one-day-seen Sir Lancelot in her heart" (l. 742). She keeps in her heart the intangible image or idea of Lancelot, while in her bedroom she guards a material keepsake, his shield.

The shield becomes a fetish to Elaine during the period of Lancelot's absence, and now it is that the opening lines of this idyll are sexually meaningful. Since Lancelot cannot be with her as a lover or as a husband, Elaine places his shield in her bedroom "where morning's earliest ray / Might strike it, and awake her with the gleam." The shield is "sacred" to her because she looks upon Lancelot as if he were a god, but also because she overvalues the shield as a fetish. That she is jealous of it and wants to be its sole possessor is seen by the fact that "day by day, / Leaving her household and good father, [she] climb'd / That eastern tower, and entering barr'd her door." Her sexual interest in the shield is manifest when she embroiders a case for it and each day behind barred doors "Stript off the case, and read the naked shield." As a fetishist, Elaine would unconsciously derive daily sexual pleasure from slipping Lancelot's shield in and out of her case. This is a classic example of Freudian symbolism. Once Elaine undresses her fetish, her stimulated imagination is allowed free play. Lancelot's masculinity and virility are uppermost in Elaine's mind:

> Now guess'd a hidden meaning in his arms,
> Now made a pretty history to herself
> Of every dint a sword had beaten in it,
> And every scratch a lance had made upon it,
> Conjecturing when and where: . . .
> And ah, God's mercy, what a stroke was there!
> And here a thrust that might have kill'd . . . .

Psychologically, Elaine would be unaware of treating Lancelot's shield as a substitute for Lancelot himself, nor would she be aware of having any sexual interest in the shield. The object truly serves the purpose of a fetish as it pleases Elaine, who "so lived in fantasy."

Lancelot and Lavaine meanwhile ride to the lists where Lancelot distinguishes himself and wins the diamond. He is severely wounded, however, and refuses the prize, thinking he will die. Before anyone can stop him, Lancelot leaves the field of combat and goes with Lavaine to a poplar grove where a hermit finds and cares for him. King Arthur sends Sir Gawain to discover the unknown knight who, save for the wearing of a lady's favor, fought like

Lancelot. Gawain is charged with giving the diamond to the knight.

But Gawain wearies of his quest until he comes to Astolat. There he tells an anxious Elaine the knight with the red sleeve won the joust and was severely wounded. "Whereat she caught her breath. / Thro' her own side she felt the sharp lance go" (l. 620). Although Gawain realizes that Elaine is in love with Lancelot, he still flirts with her until she rebuffs him by showing her shield. Gawain says King Arthur was right about the unknown jouster's being Lancelot, "And right was I," answers Elaine, "I, / Who dream'd my knight the greatest knight of all" (l. 663). She accepts the diamond from Gawain, who should not have offered it to her, and Gawain again tries to woo her before he returns to Camelot.

At court, Queen Guinevere hears of the maid of Astolat. What she hears makes her sexually jealous of Elaine. Guinevere sat "With lips severely placid, felt the knot / Climb in her throat, and with feet unseen / Crush'd the wild passion out against the floor" (ll. 735-737). Guinevere's jealousy, which suggests her distrust of Lancelot, contrasts with Elaine's loyalty to Lancelot, for as soon as she can, Elaine seeks and finds Lancelot, intending to nurse him to health. Lancelot takes the diamond from Elaine, and since "Her face was near, and as we kiss the child / That does the task assign'd, he kiss'd her face. / At once she slipt like water to the floor" (ll. 823-825).

Day after day Elaine cares for Lancelot.

> Her fine care had saved his life.
> And the sick man forgot her simple blush,
> Would call her friend and sister, sweet Elaine,
> Would listen for her coming and regret
> Her parting step, and held her tenderly,
> And loved her with all love except the love
> Of man and woman when they love their best. l. 864

Lancelot remains true to Guinevere. At times in mid-sickness he vows to purge himself of dishonor to Arthur, but "when the blood ran lustier in him again," he thinks of Guinevere. Elaine murmurs to herself, "He will not love me. How then? must I die?" (l. 888). Half the night she repeats to herself, "Must I die?" And when Lancelot is well enough to return to Astolat, Elaine tells him passionately, "I have gone mad. I love you; let me die" (l. 925). Lancelot tells her he can never marry, and Elaine says, "No, no . . . I care not to be your wife, / But to be with you still, to see your face, / To serve you, and to follow you thro' the world" (ll. 932-934). Lancelot refuses her as kindly as he can, and then one evening he sends for his shield.

For the last time, Elaine goes to her bedroom to handle her fetish. "Full meekly rose the maid, / Stript off the case, and gave the naked shield" (l. 972). Lancelot leaves without waving farewell, the one discourtesy he ever shows Elaine. "So in her tower alone the maiden sat. / His very shield was gone; only the case, / Her own poor work, her empty labor, left" (ll. 982-984). No one can comfort Elaine.

When she first began admitting to herself that Lancelot would never be hers, Elaine developed a death wish that gained expression in recurring premonitions warning her she would die. As her certainty of losing Lancelot increased, so did the premonitions increase. Lancelot could not marry her, nor would he accept her offer to be with him as an unmarried companion. And now that she has lost both Lancelot and the fetish which she had sexually associated with him, Elaine openly desires death. She writes a song that ends, "I needs must follow death, who calls for me; / Call and I follow, I follow! let me die" (ll. 1010-1011). It is as though all of the welled up sexual energy she had generated in her youth which in months past has been discharged towards Lancelot or by her lavishing sexual attention on her fetish is now turned inward to be transformed into another energy, an energy bent on death.

Elaine becomes obsessed with death. She has a priest shrive her; she makes elaborate preparations for her tomb; and within a short time she dies. Her brothers place her in a barge, where, dressed in white, she is laid on her bed. They "Set in her hand a lily, o'er her hung /The silken case with braided blazonings" (l. 1142). With the case originally meant to house her fetish now fluttering as a pennant, the barge floats down towards Camelot.

That day at the palace Sir Lancelot plans to give the nine-years-fought-for diamonds to Guinevere. But the Queen spurns his gift: "Not for me! / For her, for your new fancy" (l. 1211). She tells him, "Add my diamonds to her pearls; Deck her with these; tell her, she shines me down." Then in a rage of sexual jealousy the wild Queen takes the diamonds and flings them through an open casement. They fall into a stream

> And right across
> Where these had fallen, slowly past the barge
> Whereon the lily maid of Astolat
> Lay smiling, like a star in blackest night. l. 1235

In Elaine's hand is a letter addressed to Lancelot which tells the cause of her death:

> "Most noble lord, Sir Lancelot of the Lake,
> I, sometime call'd the maid of Astolat,
> Come, for you left me taking no farewell,
> Hither, to take my last farewell of you.
> I loved you, and my love had no return,
> And therefore my true love has been my death." l. 1269

After Lancelot tells King Arthur the whole story of his

involvement with Elaine, the King asks him to see that she is buried worshipfully. She is buried like a queen.

> Then Arthur spake among them: "Let her tomb
> Be costly, and her image thereupon,
> And let the shield of Lancelot at her feet
> Be carven, and her lily in her hand." l. 1331

The story of her voyage is emblazoned on her tomb in letters gold and azure, which are the colors that adorn Sir Lancelot's shield. With ironic propriety, Elaine will be remembered by the symbols of her fetish.

From beginning to end that fetish has significance in "Lancelot and Elaine." It is a persistent motif which helps to unify the poem; it adds psychological interest to the poem; and it allows an exploration of female sexuality. By concentrating on Lancelot's shield as the focus of sexual attention in this idyll, one begins to discover the depth of Elaine's sexual feeling for Lancelot. In effect, understanding how the shield functions as a fetish gives one an understanding of a powerful method for poetically expressing repressed sexuality. There is psychological acumen in "Lancelot and Elaine" which gives intellectual substance to its celebrated poetry.

II

Paull F. Baum has a paragraph on "Pelleas and Ettarre" in *Tennyson Sixty Years After* which begins, "The 'idyll' of Pelleas and Ettarre, when the last veil of poetical adornment has been twitched off, is one of the poorest of them all."[2] The paragraph neglects to say that beyond "poetical adornment" this idyll deals seriously with a *rite de passage,* with a young man's discovering himself and his society, with a puppet reenactment of Lancelot and Guinevere's betrayal of Arthur, and with an abundance of sexual symbolism. The sexual subject matter was recently noted by

Lawrence Poston, who compared Pelleas and Tennyson's philosopher-poet, Lucretius: "Both Lucretius, deluded by 'the sober majesties / Of settled, sweet, Epicurean life,' and Pelleas, worshipping at the wrong shrine, have denied the flesh altogether and are suddenly overcome by it when, for the first time, they must confront its claims."[3] The comparison is appropriate, and the two poems Poston draws upon have something more in common.

Tennyson wrote "Pelleas and Ettarre" about a year after he published "Lucretius," in the spring of 1868. That poem's sensuality is as well known as the fact that Lucretius drinks a philtre meant to arouse and excite him. Among the philosopher's lewd and licentious dreams is one of Helen wherein the shape of a phallus figures importantly:

> From utter gloom stood out the breasts,
> The breasts of Helen, and hoveringly a sword
> Now over and now under, now direct,
> Pointed itself to pierce, but sank down shamed
> At all that beauty. ll. 60–64

The phallic sword also figures importantly in "Pelleas and Ettarre," where there is symbolic representation of both male and female organs. ("Lancelot and Elaine" distantly suggested such a representation when Elaine as a fetishist derived sexual pleasure from slipping Lancelot's naked shield in and out of her embroidered case.) In effect, "Pelleas and Ettarre" shows as clearly as any other idyll that the *Idylls of the King* broadly explores the various possibilities of sexual expression. At times the phallic symbols in the poem become so prominent that they are evident despite the beguiling narrative clothed with "poetical adornments"; one need hardly twitch off any veils at all.

When Pelleas is first introduced, his innocence is stressed

immediately: through high doors passed "a youth, / Pelleas, and the sweet smell of the fields / Past, and the sunshine came along with him" (ll. 4-6). He naïvely says to Arthur, "Make me thy knight, because I know, Sir King, / All that belongs to knighthood, and I love" (ll. 7-8). Having heard of a tournament whose prize was a golden circlet and a knightly sword, Pelleas wants to win the golden circlet for his lady, and for himself the sword. His reasons for wanting the prize are given in a flashback.

Lately come of his inheritance, and lord of many a barren isle, Pelleas sought to find Caerleon and King Arthur. Riding in a hot sun which causes him to reel from his horse, he takes refuge on a vaguely genital-like mound:

> [he] saw
> Near him a mound of even-sloping side
> Whereon a hundred stately beeches grew,
> And here and there great hollies under them;
> But for a mile all round was open space
> And fern and heath. l. 28

Here he rests, closes his eyes, and dreams of women and his own masculine prowess:

> "O, where? I love thee, tho' I know thee not.
> For fair thou art and pure as Guinevere,
> And I will make thee with my spear and sword
> As famous—O my Queen, my Guinevere,
> For I will be thine Arthur when we meet." l. 45

Pelleas' dream is as sexually innocent as he is himself, and as uninformed. Guinevere is hardly pure, and the fame she has won from Lancelot's spear and sword is sexual, not chivalric. But Pelleas is unaware of this irony.

He wakes from the dream to the reality of Ettarre, who is traveling with her court to Caerleon. Pelleas wonders, "Is Guinevere herself so beautiful?" What attracts Pelleas is Ettarre's *fleshly* beauty: her large violet eyes, her complexion, her limbs, her mature womanhood, her slender hand, her small shape. These are key lines: "While he gazed / The beauty of her flesh abash'd the boy, / As tho' it were the beauty of her soul" (ll. 73-75). The "boy," in short, takes the physical, sexual measure of Ettarre and loses his self-possession. "For out of the waste islands had he come, / Where saving his own sisters he had known / Scarce any but the women of his isles" (ll. 82-84). The "rough wives" Pelleas knew were nothing like Ettarre.

He is so struck by the sexual attractiveness of her body that he ignores her sarcasm, scorn of him, mocking attitude, and malicious flattery. While they ride together toward Caerleon, his "chaste awe, / His broken utterances and bashfulness, / Were all a burthen to her" (ll. 105-107). But since she is bent on hearing herself proclaimed Queen of Beauty after the lists are fought, and since she sees that Pelleas is young and strong, "she thought / That peradventure he will fight for me, / And win the circlet." Therefore, when they reach the city, she takes Pelleas' hand and pointedly offers a sexual contract:

> "O the strong hand," she said,
> "See! look at mine! but wilt thou fight for me,
> And win me this fine circlet, Pelleas,
> That I may love thee?" l. 123

Pelleas quickly agrees, for his "helpless heart leapt" at the chance of loving her. She laughs, nips his hand, and flings it from her.

The golden circlet hereafter becomes associated, even identified with Ettarre. She desires it so that it may proclaim her Queen of Beauty; Pelleas wants to win it because he desires Ettarre. Late in the poem the circlet is actually used as a metonymy for Ettarre: Pelleas waits for "news of gold" (l. 349). The substitution of an associated term for Ettarre's proper name is fitting, for neither Pelleas nor Ettarre sees the golden circlet as a thing in itself, but as a sexual symbol of Ettarre. To Pelleas, it holds the promise of a union with Ettarre. Its masculine counterpart, of course, is the knightly sword to be given as a prize at the tournament along with the golden circlet. If Pelleas is to win the circlet, if he is to win Ettarre, he must also win the sword; that is, he must prove himself a man who has sexual claims on a woman by achieving the use of a masculine phallus. This Freudian reading of the circlet and sword finds considerable support as the poem progresses.

Pelleas thinks of Ettarre constantly; he cannot sleep at night "for pleasure in his blood" (l. 131), and during the day his face shines so that men who meet him wonder after him. On the morning of the jousts, which are called "The Tournament of Youth," Pelleas distinguishes himself; "by that strong hand of his / The sword and golden circlet were achieved." King Arthur, loving his young knight, has withheld his older and mightier knights from the lists in order to help Pelleas obtain his lady's love. Ettarre's face glows with pride and glory when Pelleas wins the tournament prize; "she caught the circlet from his lance, / And there before the people crown'd herself" (ll. 166-167). But she has no intention of committing herself to Pelleas.

When Guinevere asks Ettarre why she wears an "unsunny face" to Pelleas, Ettarre answers, "Had ye not held your Lancelot in your bower, / My Queen, he had not won" (ll. 175-176). Like Lancelot, Pelleas has proved he can victoriously wield a military lance and sword; unlike Lancelot, Pelleas has yet to prove he can satisfy a woman in her bower by sexually wielding a phallic sword. Thus, as Ettarre returns to her home followed by Pelleas, she says, "I cannot bide Sir Baby." She prefers "Some rough old knight who knew the worldly way" (l. 185); Pelleas is fit for "papmeat" and "old milky fables" that mothers tell their boys. Once in her castle, Ettarre orders the drawbridge raised, and "Down rang the grate of iron thro' the groove" (l. 200). She is sexually unavailable to Pelleas, who remains alone in an open field.

For more than two weeks Pelleas stays before Ettarre's castle walls. Three times she sends her three retainer knights to drive him from the walls, but each time Pelleas defeats them. His military ability with a sword is beyond question. Once he tells Ettarre he knows she is simply trying his faith until at length she will "Yield me thy love and know me for thy knight" (l. 241). But Ettarre, echoing Guinevere's complaint about King Arthur, asks her court, "How can ye bide at peace, / Affronted with his [Pelleas'] fulsome innocence?" (ll. 257-258). Again echoing Guinevere, this time on a highly idealistic level, Ettarre wonders why she cannot completely love a man who is so devoted to her: she wonders if there might be "in him / A something—was it nobler than myself?—seem'd my reproach?" (ll. 301-303). She dismisses the brief self-examination by concluding, "He is not of my kind. / He could not love me, did he know me well."

A chance witness to Pelleas' last fight with Ettarre's knights is Sir Gawain, who passes the field while bound upon solitary adventure. He learns of Pelleas' unrequited love for Ettarre, tells him, "Ye know nothing," and pledges, "by the honor of the Table Round," to tame Ettarre for Pelleas. "Hold me for your friend," he tells him (l. 332). His plan is to praise Pelleas to Ettarre "till she long / To have thee back in lusty life again" (ll. 343-344). Hoping to hear "news of gold" three nights hence, Pelleas lends Gawain his horse and arms, "saving the goodly sword, his prize" (l. 351). Pelleas does not give up his sword to Gawain, for he says, "Betray me not, but help— / Art thou not he whom men call light-of-love?" (ll. 352-353). Although willing to accept Gawain's offer to win Ettarre for him, Pelleas is sexually uneasy about the promiscuous Gawain's being with Ettarre. He keeps his sword as a symbolic retention of his own manly potential. The phallus reassures Pelleas of his manhood.

For three days he waits and wonders, "Why lingers Gawain with his golden news?" (l. 402). A lay entitled "A worm within the rose" vexes his heart, and probably vexes his mind subliminally. If the rose evokes Ettarre, the Queen of Beauty, and the worm uncomfortably evokes the penis of Gawain, who once looked at villainy and "in his heat and eagerness / Trembled and quiver'd, as the dog" (ll. 274-275), then the lay does indeed foreshadow Gawain's seduction of Ettarre. This kind of sexual symbolism anticipates the symbolic image of a genital orifice which Pelleas comes upon when he eventually rides to Ettarre's castle to find "Wide open were the gates" (l. 405) and "the postern portal also wide / Yawning" (l. 411). A phallic scramble "up a slope of garden" with "brambles mixt / and overgrowing" brings Pelleas to "three pavilions rear'd / Above the bushes, gilden-peakt" (ll. 412-420). The erect pavilions signal the revels of Ettarre's knights and damsels, "And in the third, the circlet of the jousts / Bound on her brow, were Gawain and Ettarre" (ll. 425-426).

The sexual symbolism continues: Pelleas draws back "as a hand that pushes thro' the leaf / To find a nest and feels a snake" (ll. 427-428). The bush, nest, womb images are as consistent as the worm, snake, penis images. Pelleas creeps through the court

> Fingering at his sword-handle until he stood
> There on the castle-bridge once more, and thought,
> "I will go back, and slay them where they lie." l. 435

While Gawain sexually enjoys Ettarre, Pelleas can do no

more physically than finger at his sword-handle. His impotence is in fine contrast to Gawain's sexual competency.

Finally, Pelleas returns to Ettarre's pavilion

> and groaning laid
> The naked sword athwart their naked throats,
> There left it, and them sleeping; and she lay,
> The circlet of the tourney round her brows,
> And the sword of the tourney across her throat. 1. 446

Pelleas mounts his horse, stares again at the penially erect towers, "larger than themselves / In their own darkness," and rides off. His sexual frustration is evident as he "crush'd the saddle with his thighs, and clench'd / His hands, and madden'd with himself and moan'd" (ll. 450-451). Equally evident is his sexually motivated rage.

He wishes that while he gazed the huge, solid towers would shiver to their base and split, that the harlot roofs would burst. Unable to prove himself sexually, Pelleas now wants to see sexual destruction.

> Let the fierce east scream thro' your eyelet-holes,
> And whirl the dust of harlots round and round
> In dung and nettles! hiss, snake— 1. 462

He calls himself a fool for loving Ettarre, and then with illuminating honesty calls himself "beast too."

> Love?—we be all alike; only the King
> Hath made us fools and liars. O noble vows!
> O great and sane and simple race of brutes
> That own no lust because they have no law. 1. 472

He concludes, "I never loved her, I but lusted for her—" (1. 475) and the reader recalls Pelleas' first sight of Ettarre: "The beauty of her flesh abash'd the boy, / As tho' it were the beauty of her soul" (ll. 74-75). These lines give weight to all conjecture about sexuality in

"Pelleas and Ettarre," for if Pelleas ever deceived himself in thinking his love for Ettarre was pure, noble, and spiritual, he now accepts the fact of his carnal appetite for the woman from the moment he saw her. In his innocence, in his sexual adolescence, he never loved Ettarre; he but lusted for her.

Ettarre finds out "that her ever-veering fancy turn'd / To Pelleas" when she discovers his sword on her throat. It is too late, however, for Pelleas to be her "one true knight on earth / And only lover." She pines for him, "desiring him in vain" (ll. 483-486). Pelleas has ridden half the night to a monastery.

In a dream, Pelleas sees that Sir Gawain will betray King Arthur by destroying Camelot itself: "Gawain fired / The Hall of Merlin, and the morning star / Reel'd in the smoke, brake into flame, and fell" (ll. 507-509). The monk Percivale tells Pelleas when he wakes that Arthur has indeed been betrayed, betrayed by Lancelot and Guinevere. And it fares with Pelleas

> as with one
> Who gets a wound in battle, and the sword
> That made it plunges thro' the wound again,
> And pricks it deeper. l. 521

Information of Guinevere's adultery and Lancelot's false behavior completes Pelleas' sexual education, and he has had enough of the phallic sword.

Pelleas flees Percivale and rides towards Camelot, where he encounters Lancelot riding airily, "Warm with a gracious parting from the Queen" (l. 447). Pelleas shouts, "A scourge am I / To lash the treasons of the Table Round" (l. 554). He cries,

> "I am wrath and shame and hate and evil fame,
> And like a poisonous wind I pass to blast
> And blaze the crime of Lancelot and the Queen." l. 558

When Pelleas falls after closing with Lancelot, he tells Guinevere's lover, "Thou art false as hell; slay me, I have no sword" (l. 564). By now the line "I have no sword" is rife with meaning, and lest one overlook its significance, or mistakenly believe it has only military relevance, the line is shortly repeated word for word in an entirely different situation.

Lancelot spares Pelleas' life, although Pelleas shrieks, "My will is to be slain" (l. 567). They make their separate ways to the great hall of Camelot, where Guinevere, surrounded by her knights and dames, questions them about their fight. She reproaches Pelleas for not chivalrously accepting a fall from the great Lancelot, and then wonders if Pelleas has other griefs. Guinevere offers to help him if she can.

> But Pelleas lifted up an eye so fierce
> She quail'd; and he, hissing "I have no sword,"
> Sprang from the door into the dark. l. 591

The Queen catches his meaning instantly, looks hard upon her lover, and he on her, "And each foresaw the dolorous day to be." All talk dies, and silence comes upon the hall.

Pelleas has publicly confronted both Lancelot and Guinevere with the fact of their sexual attachment to each other. What he says in effect is this: despite the trappings of knighthood, where vows have chivalric meaning and the knightly sword betokens valor, gallantry, and gentlemanly conduct, the society of Camelot harbors sexual betrayal and a phallicly oriented way of life. To conform to this way of life means that one has to countenance the sexual promiscuity of a Lancelot or Gawain, a Guinevere or Ettarre. Pelleas refuses to accept such a carnal society—he not only surrenders his sword, but he reproaches others with the statement that he has no sword. Through distasteful experience Pelleas has found that idealistic belief in knighthood comes tragically undone when it confronts the destructive energy of sexual lust.

If being a man in King Arthur's Britain means living by the phallic sword, then Pelleas wishes to be slain. Even Percivale in this idyll gossips about royal adultery. "Pelleas and Ettarre" clearly shows the moral decadence of society; the poem shows evil through the eyes of an innocent who eventually finds his own innocence sullied by sexual lust. What the poem does not do is show how innocence, nobility, chivalry, or even spiritual love can maintain its essential character when man lacks the ability to distinguish the beauty of the flesh from the beauty of the soul. This is the intellectual failing of the poem. As in all of the idylls, however, "Pelleas and Ettarre" does say that promiscuity, lust, and erotic love are ruinous, for "love is worthy, or valid, only when it is based on something higher than love, only when it serves as a stimulus to "right moral action."[4] Clyde Ryals makes this point in his recent collection of essays on *Idylls of the King, From the Great Deep*. Both "Lancelot and Elaine" and "Pelleas and Ettarre" support Ryals' general conclusion that "Tennyson never praises married, or any other kind of, love as an end in itself. With Wordsworth he recognizes that 'Unless this love by a still higher love / Be hallowed,' unless it be 'By Heaven inspired,' it is 'but delight how pitiable' (*The Prelude,* Bk. XIV)." The idylls recognize the complex problems which attend the relationship of sexuality and love, and if they do not solve the problems, they nevertheless achieve distinction by powerfully using symbolism to suggest the intricacy of man's sexual nature.

5
Spasmodic Poetry

The two foregoing chapters dealt with well-known poems by major authors. Today, only advanced students of English literature doing highly specialized work read the Spasmodic school of poets, and yet this school was important in Victorian England for roughly fifteen years, from the late 1830's through the early 1850's. People then were reading Philip James Bailey, J. Westland Marston, Richard Hengist Horne, Ebenezer Jones, John Stanyan Bigg, Alexander Smith, and Sydney Dobell. Graduate students know these poets today for little more than having influenced Alfred Tennyson's *Maud* (1855) and Elizabeth Barrett Browning's *Aurora Leigh* (1856). In the study of literary culture entitled *The Victorian Temper,* Jerome Buckley had to remind his audience pointedly that the Spasmodic poets once assumed considerable proportions: "They once cast so long a shadow across the whole verse of their time that their frenetic volumes cannot even now be quite ignored in any estimate of early Victorian taste."[1]

Buckley's use of the word "frenetic" to describe the work of the Spasmodic poets is in keeping with his calling the school "Byronic" and its poetry opulent or fleshly or "inflamed by borrowed passions." Passion is indeed the catchword used to tag Spasmodic poetry: it has not only turbulent passions and surging passions, but it has also "passion piled on passion," or so Hugh Walker described it in *The Literature of the Victorian Era* (1910). With regard to the particular emotions aroused by sexual feeling, there are still observations to be made as to how the Spasmodic poets expressed sexuality and how they managed to deal with the problems caused by sexual repression. A sampling which spans the years during which the Spasmodic school was in vogue might pay attention to Philip James Bailey's *Festus* (1839), Ebenezer Jones's work in *Studies of Sensation and Event* (1843), and Alexander Smith's *A Life-Drama* (1853).[2]

In *Festus,* Philip Bailey had every opportunity to explore whatever emotions he wished to explore. The forty thousand lines of his epic-drama cover literally hundreds of pages and place the hero, Festus, in dozens of situations in various locales with many different characters. But mostly Festus talks. At times he sounds like Marlowe's Faustus or Goethe's Faust: "My spirit is on edge. I can enjoy / Nought which has not the honied sting of sin." Yet when it comes to action, when it comes to experiencing life, Festus proves to be of questionable descent. His namesakes lived through what Festus talks about in the third person:

> His heart's passions made him oft do that
> Which made him writhe to think on what he had done,
> And thin his blood by weeping at a night.
> If madness wrought the sin, the sin wrought madness,
> And made a round of ruin.

The Faustus family line peters out in Festus, despite this promise of life: "Rouse thee, heart; / Bow of my life thou yet art full of spring! / My quiver still hath many purposes." If there is a sexual word play on "quiver," it is merely pretentious boasting.

When Lucifer raises the female spirit of Angela, Festus says to her, "Dear art thou to me now, as in that hour / When first Love's wave of feeling, spray-like broke / Into bright utterance, and we said we loved." Since feeling first broke into *utterance,* and they *said* they loved, there is reason to suspect Festus' report to Lucifer about Angela:

> She fell upon me like a snow-wreath thawing.
> Never were bliss and beauty, love and woe,
> Ravelled and twined together into madness,
> As in that one wild hour.

Festus forgets that a gentleman never tells, and the odd sexual simile he uses is richly graphic. Later in the poem he again uses snow to construct a sexual image:

> Then as tired wanderer, snow-blinded, sinks
> And swoons upon the swelling drift, and dies,
> So on her dazzling bosom would he lay
> His famished lips, and end their travels there.

Festus says these lines to Helen, who is another character Bailey makes partial to sexual figures of speech.

Helen tells Festus, "I cannot live away from thee. How can / A flower live without its root?" When Festus ignores her, she speaks to a piano in sexual terms designed to win back Festus' attention. "Sweet! I come," she says. "What a time / Since I have touched thine eloquent white fingers." The similes follow: the piano is

> like a bud
> Of unborn sweets, and thick about the heart
> With ripe and rosy beauty—full to trembling.
> I love it like a sister. Hark!—its tones;
> They melt the soul within one like a sword,
> Albeit sheathed, by lightning.

In truth, she might as well make love to the piano rather than to Festus. As far as he is concerned, there is little point to seeing a quiver as other than a quiver, a root as other than a root, a sword as other than a sword.

The height of Festus' passion in this long, long poem comes when he makes love to Elissa. His speech to her is theatrical and full of high-flown adolescent sexual bombast:

> Be mine! be me! be aught but so far
> Give me thyself! It is not enough for me,
> That I have gazed and doted on thee till
> Mine eye is dazzled and my brain is dizzied:
> Thou must exhaust all senses; not enough
> That in long dreams my soul hath spread itself
> Like water over every living line
> Of this sweet make, dreaming thou was all lips;
> Nor that it now sinks in the face of thee,
> Like a sea-sunset, hot and tired with the long,
> Long day of love;—it is not enough. I must
> Have more—have all! For I have sworn to fill
> Mine arms with bliss—thus—thus—thus!

Sexual expression in *Festus* never really does get past the adolescent stage. Despite his passionate rhetoric, Festus is remarkably restrained. Philip James Bailey is unwilling or unable to do more with sexual material than lead up to it and then talk around it. And yet the similes and metaphors in the poem that seemingly conceal sexual expression indicate the presence of sexually repressed emotions in *Festus.*

There is another tale to tell, however, about the poetry of Ebenezer Jones. With reference to *Studies of Sensation and Event* (1843), Professor Buckley said, "In his writing Jones sought release from the rigorous Calvinism of his childhood and the poverty and disease that overshadowed his maturity. But his defiant pursuit of passion led only to a deliberate and circumstantial sensuousness."[3] Two of Jones's poems, "Emily" and "Zingalee," deserve a stronger term than "sensuous" to describe their content, for they both indulge a sexual appetite with sensuality that is almost lewd. It is obvious that Jones's verse deliberately cultivates sex appeal; the sexual elements are central and essential. One of the most interesting things about Jones's handling of sex, especially in "Emily," is how far he takes his Victorian flirtation with the techniques of pornography.

The poem "Emily" is, of course, not pornographic. There is no surface intent to arouse sexual desire in a reader. In fact, any Victorian reader who was aroused would blame himself and not the poem. He would feel that sexual stimulation came from his own mind, not from the page he was reading. And yet "Emily" is not quite so innocent. The poem tells of a man who spies on a young girl as she lies on a robe in a forest glade. The man describes the girl's actions, and then goes to her. She stays with him a short time and quickly runs away. What makes the poem a sexual tease is that the man, a peeping Tom if not a voyeur, describes Emily as she lies caressing herself while the wind lifts her clothing. The way the speaker talks about Emily's posture and movements prompt the imagination to consider the possibility that the girl might be masturbating. Here are the opening lines of the poem:

> Oh! listen, nymphs! to my distress;
> Tell Emily! tell what wild desire
> Throbs all my veins, and yet confess
> I would not lose the glorious fire.
> Oh listen, nymphs! in sunny wind,
> Emily on the lawn reclined;
> One of her beauteous arms was wound,
> Embracingly her pillow round;
> Her face and bosom, 'neath the sky,
> Backwardly lolled in smiles did lie;
> Her face and bosom upward bending
> Flushed as with virgin shames; and lending
> Her hand to some caressing dream,
> Over her flowing limbs it lay,
> Where stricken by the sunny beam,

Around it rosy lights did play:
And seemed those gently swelling limbs,
Curving at sound of warm love-hymns,
Towards fond minglement, though they
Minglement made not, but did stray
Partedly ever;—and the dress
Which fell soft o'er this loveliness,
Its glowing life all unconcealing,
Yet shaded from entire revealing—
With witching modesty, confessing
What matchless splendor still it veiled,
Though oft the breezes, rudely pressing,
The heavenly secrecy assailed,—
And then illumined the couch of azure,
And then the air did pant and glow,
While shivering with mysterious pleasure,
Like waves her limbs did lift and flow.

The scene has several trappings of a peepshow: the spectator is allowed to watch the girl as she caresses her "gently swelling limbs," but he cannot touch her; the girl's dress is arranged so that it reveals her body, but not entirely—"Though oft the breezes, rudely pressing, / The heavenly secrecy assailed." The pathetic fallacy says it is the narrator of the scene and not the air that did "pant and glow" as the girl, "shivering with mysterious pleasure," moves her body so that "her limbs did lift and flow." If there is any doubt, if there can be any doubt, that the man watching Emily is sexually stimulated by her, the doubt must be dispelled by the man's action as soon as Emily leaves:

Upon that ground her robe was spread,
And on that robe was lain my head;
Into its folds, burningly yearning,
My lips went, pouring kisses, till
I shook with ecstasy.

In an embarrassing display of sexual frustration, he buries

his cheek in the pillow where Emily had pressed her cheek. The robe and pillow, not in themselves erotic objects, take on the sexual attractions of a fetish—they receive the sexual attention that the man wants to give to Emily.

The poem "Zingalee" is more directly sexual than "Emily," and far less interesting. A husband home from the war looks for his wife, Zingalee. Anxious to see her, excited by the thought of her, "He enters the mansion, with quivering frame / He glides to her chamber." At precisely that moment, Zingalee happens to be in bed with a lover.

> There, in voluptuous gloom,
> Her breasts all naked, and heaving,
> Lay his bride;
> And her beside,
> One like a man, around him cleaving
> Her quivering limbs, while still she moaned grieving,
> "I cannot even die from thee parted."

The husband faints, recovers, and runs to a garden near the house. In strangely archaic language, the narrator says, "He gnashes his teeth, and teareth bare / His bosom, and grovelleth on the ground / His naked flesh, and howleth around." Then the husband recalls sexual exploits he had with Zingalee when she, "Some robeless nymph, sported with flowers." He immediately checks himself: "But another burns at each naked grace." Unable to bear the thought of someone else burning at Zingalee's naked grace, the man runs over brown pastures to die on a moor. The narrator ends the poem telling Zingalee not to weep, but to dance and exult with her live lover.

This poem, like "Emily," has a woman at its center who has only sexual meaning for the male character. Emily and Zingalee are sensually described and sexually desired by men who are excited as they watch from a distance and see the women in erotic situations. Since the male Victorian reader would adopt the point of view and perhaps identify with the male spectator in each of the poems, the women, especially Emily, might well arrest the interest of a reader's repressed sexual longing. Emily is a sister one century removed of the heroines in cheap modern novels who sexually excite readers in the safety of their armchairs. Zingalee, "her breasts all naked, and heaving," with her "quivering limbs" wrapped around a man—this Zingalee has hardly any literary interest, but she could appeal in a small way to male readers who had yet to meet the female conquests of a James Bond.

There is sexual play of a different sort in Alexander Smith's *A Life-Drama* (1853). The hero of Smith's poem, a poet named Walter, has an erotic sensibility which expresses itself in variously perverse ways. For example, as the poem develops Walter's attitude towards poetry, it becomes clear that he is in sexual pursuit of the Muse. At the beginning of *A Life-Drama,* Walter says,

> For Poesy my heart and pulses beat,
> For Poesy my blood runs red and fleet;
> As Moses' serpent the Egyptians' swallowed,
> One passion eats the rest. My soul is followed
> By strong ambition to out-roll a lay.

After this emotional declaration, he continues his wooing:

> Poesy! Poesy! I'd give to thee,
> As passionately, my rich-laden years,
> My bubble pleasures, and my awful joys,
> As Hero gave her trembling sighs to find
> Delicious death on wet Leander's lip.

Only an erotic attraction to poetry would make Walter say that he longs to hang "O'er the fine pants and trembles of a line" of verse.

But Walter's attraction to poetry is as a Hero to a Leander, as a woman to a man. When the Muse does not accept the offer of his rich-laden years, Walter says, "As well may some wild maiden waste her love / Upon the calm front of a marble Jove." Walter sees himself as a wild maiden and the Muse as a marble Jove. Here, then, Walter plays a feminine role; furthermore, he consistently lacks a normal male identity with normal male drives throughout the poem. An abundance of lines gives evidence of this perversity.

Figures of speech constantly suggest Walter's femininity. He says in an apostrophe to Poetry, "I love thee, Poesy! Thou art a rock; / I, a weak wave, would break on thee and die!" And when a Lady looks at him as he sleeps in a forest, she compares him metaphorically to a flower: "I've seen full many a flower, / But never one so fair. A lovely youth, / With dainty cheeks, and ringlets like a girl." Walter himself tells of how "the dark dumb Earth / Lay on her back" and then he identifies with the feminine figure of Earth while telling of his relationship with another poet: "He was the sun, I was that squab—the earth." With a change in geography, Walter returns to a sea metaphor: "O! he was rich, / And I rejoiced upon his shore of pearls, / A weak enamored sea." This feminine identification with the sea again occurs as Walter writes a poem for a Lady. His subject is "A silent isle on which the love-sick sea / Dies with faint kisses and a murmured joy." The pathetic fallacy indicates that Walter projects his own emotions onto "The passion-panting sea;" various similes and metaphors indicate that sexually he adopts a female point of view.

This point of view changes when Walter grows old, but he retains his erotic sensibility and a perverse choice of love objects. Grown old and gray, Walter yearns for "that child so fair, / That infant in her golden hair." He tells us,

> My head is gray, my blood is young,
> Red-leaping in my veins,

> The spring doth stir my spirit yet
> To seek the cloistered violet.

A young girl stirs his spirit:

> I gazéd till my heart grew wild,
> To fold her in my warm caresses,
> Clasp her showers of golden tresses,—
> O, dreamy-eyéd child!

By leaving England to forget the child, Walter avoids the possibility of a direct sexual encounter. Upon his return home, he finds the child has died.

Walter's last love affair is with a woman named Violet. Here he once again adopts a feminine identity: "O God! I'd be the very floor that bears / Such a majestic thing!" When he makes love to Violet, she adopts a masculine posture at his request: "Bend over me, my Beautiful, my Own. / O, I could lie with face upturned forever." None of these affairs taken singly necessarily reveals the nature of Walter's sexual disturbance. Considered in a series of romantic encounters, however, the affairs emphasize Walter's life-long inability to assume sexually normal male roles.

Alexander Smith's *A Life-Drama* contains a good many lines which express sexual emotion. Sexuality in Smith, however, generally takes forms that blur male and female identities. The male hero of Smith's poem has sexual desires which are directed towards peculiar love-objects, such as a masculine Muse of poetry and a golden-haired, dreamy-eyed child. But sexual perversity in the poem is not immediately obvious because it is frequently hidden by figurative language. One cannot easily ponder the implications of similes and metaphors or try to keep images in mind in order to consider the overall patterns they form since the very length of *A Life-Drama* makes it difficult to remember the particular elements of its overall structure. Nevertheless, there is a definite sexual motif which underlies the poem.

One looks in vain, however, for a sexual theme or a manner of sexual expression that might unite Philip James Bailey, Ebenezer Jones, and Alexander Smith. As a school, the Spasmodic poets can be loosely characterized by reference to their overexcited style, fustian, rant, and a general lack of formal discipline. But not even a loose generalization can be safely made about their handling of sex. Bailey is more reticent than the other two, more likely to write about nonsexual kinds of passion. Jones, on the other hand, makes no attempt to avoid the subject of sex. "Emily" and "Zingalee" sexually tease the imagination. Alexander Smith puzzles the imagination; *A Life-Drama* has more homosexual than bisexual overtones. All in all, Bailey, Jones, and Smith express themselves sexually with individual voices, each in a minor key. The quality of the poets' sexual expression warrants scant attention, but their work cannot be ignored because of its historical importance. Collectively, the poets give evidence that the Spasmodic school did not subscribe to a common sexual curriculum; individually, each has written poetry which offers interesting challenges to the psychological critic.

6

Charles Dickens; Orphans, Incest, and Repression

Charles Dickens' novels have given rise to such an enormous number of critical articles and books that it is becoming virtually impossible to read each newly printed work. Ada Nisbet's recent bibliographic survey of Dickens in *Victorian Fiction: A Guide to Research* is selective and mostly concerned with material published during the past quarter of a century, and yet her survey covers more than one hundred tightly printed pages.[1] Any retrenchment is out of the question, because important ways of looking at Dickens are being constantly discovered, and the forthcoming Pilgrim edition of his letters will surely stimulate much additional criticism. One way of taking profitable advantage of what has been done and of what is being done, however, is to combine areas in Dickens scholarship that will form new boundaries of significance.

The subject of orphans in Dickens' novels has long been extremely well covered by critics. The subject of incest, on the other hand, has received relatively scant attention, and truly notable studies of incest in Dickens have not appeared until this decade. My purpose here is to juxtapose the two subjects, giving brief notice to the orphans in Dickens followed by a more extensive discussion of incest. The significance of the two subjects will then be discussed separately before being finally related to the topic of sexual repression in Dickens' novels.

In short, the following pages consider what orphans and incest have to do with sexual repression when the subjects are viewed collectively.

The first stage of the synthesis gets underway by establishing the fact that in any Dickens novel there are an extraordinary number of orphans. For example, in *Martin Chuzzlewit* the young people without parents are Martin, Mark Tapley, John Westlock, Tom and Ruth Pinch, and Mary Graham; Jonas Chuzzlewit, who tries to kill his father, has no mother; and neither do Charity and Mercy Pecksniff. Among those lacking one or both parents in *Dombey and Son* are Paul and Florence Dombey, Walter Gay, Edith Granger, Alice Marwood, and Mr. P. Toots.

George Ford has compiled this list of orphans in *David Copperfield*:

> Those who in childhood have lost both parents include David himself who becomes "an orphan in the wide world" at an early age, as well as Emily, Traddles, the Orfling who is attached to the Micawbers, Mrs. Copperfield, Martha Endell ("early left fatherless and motherless"), and Rosa Dartle. Those who in childhood have lost one parent, the half-orphans as they might be called, include Steerforth, Uriah Heep, Annie Strong (whose husband she admires as a 'father' for herself), Agnes, and Dora. The last named, having lost her remaining parent during the course of the story, is referred to thereafter by Agnes as "the orphan child."[2]

Professor Ford momentarily forgets that Ham also belongs on his list.

In an article entitled "Parents and Children in *Great Expectations*," Vereen Bell writes,

> Some of the children [in *Great Expectations*] are orphans, either utterly alone or dominated brutally by parent surrogates; the ones who are not orphans have parents who are either grotesque and domineering or witless and incompetent. Not one of these children has the parent he needs,

> and no parent provides the love and mature guidance he is meant to. In *Great Expectations* this pattern is clearer because the context is less cluttered, but of course all of Dickens' novels are the same way.[3]

An alert reader cannot fail to notice that for all practical purposes a remarkable number of Dickens' literary children and their natural parents have no relationship. Scores of Dickens' characters are, either literally or figuratively, orphans.

But even an alert reader may miss the incest theme which appears in Dickens' novels several times over. Critics have only recently begun to write about incest in Dickens and yet his novels have been read for several generations. Discussion of the oversight is momentarily less important than actually calling attention to the far-reaching theme.

In a seminal essay simply called "Charles Dickens," George Orwell wrote in 1939 of an "incestuous atmosphere" which provides the Dickens novel with its ideal ending. Orwell wrote, "It is perfectly attained in *Nicholas Nickleby, Martin Chuzzlewit,* and *Pickwick,* and it is approximated to in varying degrees in almost all the others."[4] None of the novels is closely analyzed in this light, but in *Charles Dickens, The World of His Novels* J. Hillis Miller specifically drew upon Orwell with reference to the ending of *Martin Chuzzlewit.* Noting that Tom Pinch and his sister Ruth are relatively close, Miller said, "This relation is the kind of thing that made it possible for George Orwell to talk about incestuous domestic relationships in Dickens' novels." Miller actually has no occasion to support his borrowed thesis, but it is fitting to say that Tom and Ruth Pinch have an "incestuous domestic relationship."[5] Theirs is perhaps the most innocent of such affairs in Dickens, and yet the couple deserve passing notice because the hint of incest in *Martin Chuzzle-*

wit (1844) looks forward to profoundly involved incestuous affairs in later novels.

The woman Tom Pinch would have liked to live with is Mary Graham. He first admires one of "the loveliest and most beautiful faces you can possibly picture to yourself" when Mary listens to him playing the organ in a village church. Tom plays the organ for Mary several times. "To have given her but a minute's pleasure every day," Tom says, "I would have gone on playing the organ at those times until I was an old man" (V). And that organ, incidentally, is once used in a metaphoric sense with sexual overtones which convey a measure of Mary's attraction for Tom. The narrator of *Martin Chuzzlewit* tells us that Tom dreamed of running away with Mary Graham, for the more he saw of her, the more he admired her beauty, her intelligence, and her other charms: "When she spoke, Tom held his breath, so eagerly he listened; when she sang, he sat like one entranced. She touched his organ, and from that bright epoch, even it, the old companion of his happiest hours, incapable as he had thought of elevation, began a new and deified existence" (XXIV). But Mary Graham is meant for young Martin Chuzzlewit, and Tom is meant for his sister Ruth.

When Tom sees Ruth after a long absence, he finds her quite as sexually attractive as he found Mary:

> "Why, bless my soul!" said Tom, looking at her with great pride, when they had tenderly embraced each other, "how altered you are, Ruth! I should scarcely have known you, my love, if I had seen you anywhere else, I declare! You are so improved," said Tom, with inexpressible delight: "you are so womanly; you are so—positively, you know, you are so handsome!" (XXXVI)

They decide to find lodgings together, and from the moment of their decision Tom and Ruth Pinch are treated as newlyweds. They search for a cheap neighborhood in

Islington "quite as happily as if they had just stepped out of a snug little house of their own, to look for lodgings on account of somebody else."

A small old-fashioned house suits them, and it was a goodly sight

> to behold Tom and his sister trotting round to the baker's, and the butcher's, and the grocer's, with a kind of dreadful delight in the unaccustomed cares of housekeeping; taking secret counsel together as they gave their small orders, and distracted by the least suggestion on the part of the shopkeeper! When they got back to the triangular parlour, and Tom's sister, bustling to and fro, busy about a thousand pleasant nothings, stopped every now and then to give old Tom a kiss, or smile upon him, Tom rubbed his hands as if all Islington were his. (XXXVI)

Tom expresses his delight in the thought, "I am quite a family man all at once." Like any young husband, he tells himself, "If I can only get something to do, how comfortable Ruth and I may be!"

He does find work, and Tom and Ruth are obviously very comfortable. "She saw nothing but Tom; . . . he had never been so happy in his life" (XXXVII). Ruth is a tidy, bustling housekeeper who acts like any young housewife. She washes breakfast cups "chatting away the whole time, and telling Tom all sorts of anecdotes"; she makes the room as neat as herself—"you must not suppose its shape was half as neat as hers though, or anything like it"—and she brushes Tom's hat, sews his shirt collar, and takes him shopping to the butcher. "Off they trotted, arm-in-arm, as nimbly as you please; saying to each other what a quiet street it was to lodge in, and how very cheap, and what an airy situation" (XXXIX).

Ruth tries new recipes, and Tom teases her about her cooking abilities. They stroll together a good deal, walking arm in arm about town, and Ruth takes to calling for

Tom after work. It comes as somewhat of a surprise near the end of the novel to learn that Ruth plans to marry Tom's friend, John Westlock, but since the three young people agree to live together after the marriage, Ruth and Tom will not greatly change their lives together. Here, then, is the "incestuous atmosphere" Orwell wrote about. Here is the "incestuous domestic relationship" to which J. Hillis Miller referred. The novel which succeeds *Martin Chuzzlewit* (1844), however, makes much more of the bond between brother and sister.

In the background of *Dombey and Son* (1848) is a relationship parallel to that of Tom and Ruth Pinch in the association of John and Harriet Carker. The brother and sister innocently live together for years, and when Harriet marries Mr. Morfin in the final pages of the novel, it is clear that her brother John will form a *ménage à trois.* But in the foreground of *Dombey and Son* there is a complicated incestuous relationship which involves sexual attraction in a subdued, halting way that anticipates the outright sexuality between Tom and Louisa Gradgrind in the later novel, *Hard Times* (1854). The first person to deal with "incestuous longing" in *Dombey and Son* at any length was Mark Spilka.[6]

Among the lines Spilka uses in *Dickens and Kafka* (1963) to show the affection of Paul Dombey for his sister Florence are these:

> "Ha!" said Doctor Blimber. "Shall we make a man of him?" . . .
> "I had rather be a child," replied Paul.
> "Indeed!" said the Doctor. "Why?"
> The child sat on the table looking at him, with a curious expression of suppressed emotion in his face, and beating one hand proudly on his knee as if he had the rising tears beneath it, and crushed them. But his other hand strayed a little way the while, a little farther—farther from him yet—until it lighted on the neck of Florence. "This is why," it

> seemed to say, and then the steady look was broken up and gone; the working lip was loosened; and the tears came streaming forth. (XI)

Paul tells us he would like to go to the country with Florence "and live there with her all my life." And later, on his deathbed, Paul makes it clear that he loves Florence better than anyone else in his life. Spilka says, "At his death there is almost a consummation between them, and the identification between Florence and his mother is strikingly confirmed." This is a key passage:

> "Now lay me down," he said, "and Floy, come close to me, and let me see you!"
>
> Sister and brother wound their arms around each other, and the golden light came streaming in, and fell upon them, locked together.
>
> "How fast the river runs, between its green banks and the rushes, Floy! But it's very near the sea. I hear the waves! They always said so!"
>
> Presently he told her that the motion of the boat upon the stream was lulling him to rest. How green the banks were now, how bright the flowers growing on them, and how tall the rushes! Now the boat was out at sea, but gliding smoothly on. And now there was a shore before him. Who stood on the bank!—
>
> He put his hands together, as he had been used to do at his prayers. He did not remove his arms to do it; but they saw him fold them so, behind her neck.
>
> "Mama is like you, Floy. I know her by the face!" (XVI)

Although Paul and Florence are both very young, Spilka notices "the central stream of emotion seems to flow between adults, from whom it channels outward into peripheral relationships; at its core, moreover, it seems to involve the very sexual feelings which the Victorians repressed." Paul Dombey's affection for his sister, Spilka says, is "bathetic and incestuous."

There is no more in *Dickens and Kafka* on the subject

of incest in *Dombey and Son.* Professor Spilka does fine work taking his reading to the point of Paul's death, but he might well have traced the subject to the very close of Dickens' novel. After Paul dies, there is ample evidence of Flo's incestuous feeling for her brother, and it is interesting to note how that feeling merges with her romantic, sexual feeling toward her lover and future husband, Walter Gay.

With reference to her brother, Flo tells Walter, "He liked you very much, and said before he died that he was fond of you, and said 'Remember Walter!' and if you'll be a brother to me, Walter, now that he is gone and I have none on earth, I'll be your sister all my life, and think of you like one wherever we may be" (XIX)! Although Walter accepts Flo's idealistic offer of a brother-sister relationship, he also has more mundane thoughts: "He could calmly think how beautiful she was, how full of promise, what a home some happy man would find in such a heart one day." But Flo insists upon her terms:

> "Walter," she said, looking full upon him with her affectionate eyes, "like you, I hope for better things. I will pray for them, and believe that they will arrive. I made this little gift for Paul. Pray take it with my love, and do not look at it until you are gone away. And now, God bless you, Walter! never forget me. You are my brother, dear!" (XIX)

Shortly thereafter Walter sails to the West Indies, to be absent from the novel for hundreds of pages.

Flo eventually comes to think he has drowned at sea. When Walter actually does return, Captain Cuttle mischievously keeps him from Flo while he teases the girl about her feelings. Flo, emotionally upset, confuses the memory of Walter with her memory of Paul:

> "Ah! If I had him for my brother now!" cried Florence.
> "Don't! don't take on, my pretty!" said the Captain, "awast

> to obleege me! He *was* your nat'ral born friend like, warn't he, Pet?" Florence had no words to answer with. She only said, "Oh, dear, dear Paul! oh, Walter!" (XLIX)

The confused identity of Paul and Walter, brother and lover, is hardly set right when Walter Gay appears:

> She had no thought of him but as a brother, a brother rescued from the grave; a shipwrecked brother saved and at her side; and rushed into his arms. In all the world, he seemed to be her hope, her comfort, refuge, natural protector. "Take care of Walter, I was fond of Walter!" The dear remembrance of the plaintive voice that said so, rushed upon her soul, like music in the night. "Oh welcome home, dear Walter! Welcome to this stricken breast!" She felt the words, although she could not utter them, and held him in her pure embrace. (XLIX)

Even as that pure embrace becomes a fructifying marital embrace, Flo thinks constantly of her brother, and her husband is perfectly aware of the fact (LVII). The baby born to Walter and Florence Gay is inevitably named Paul.

Incest in *Dombey and Son* is felt more strongly than in *Martin Chuzzlewit,* and yet the incestuous bond is stronger still in Dickens' next novel, *David Copperfield* (1850). It is now commonplace for critics to point out how close the resemblance is between Clara Copperfield, David's mother, and Dora Copperfield, David's first wife; in college classrooms each year professors must suggest one way or another that David Copperfield's oedipal interest in his mother is gratified by his marrying Dora Spenlow.[7] There are no quotations from the critics, however, which are quite as telling in showing the incest motif in *David Copperfield* as the text of the novel itself.

When David was born, his father had been dead for six months, and the boyhood years were among the happiest in David's life, a time during which he was, as it were, the only man in his mother's life. Clara was "a wax doll" (I), a virtual baby who gave birth to a baby (XIII). "My mother was," David says, "unusually youthful in appearance even for her years; she hung her head, as if it were her fault, poor thing, and said, sobbing, that indeed she was afraid she was but a childish widow, and would be but a childish mother if she lived" (I). She knows nothing about keeping house, she cries a good deal, and she cannot handle figures. "I am sure we never had a word of difference respecting it, except when Mr. Copperfield objected to my threes and fives being too much like each other, or to my putting curly tails to my sevens and nines" (I). Her idea of being a good mother is to dote upon her son and lavish affection upon him.

David has his "little bed in a closet within [his] mother's room" (II) and he remembers how once she tucked him in at night when "we kissed one another over and over again, and I soon fell fast asleep" (II). He also remembers his mother as a man might remember a young wife in the flush of girlish beauty:

> Can I say of her face—altered as I have reason to remember it, perished as I know it is—that it is gone, when here it comes before me at this instant, as distinct as any face that I may choose to look on in a crowded street? Can I say of her innocent and girlish beauty, that it faded, and was no more, when its breath falls on my cheek now, as it fell that night? Can I say she ever changed, when my remembrance brings her back to life, thus only; and, truer to its loving youth than I have been, or man ever is, still holds fast what it cherished then? (II)

This visual memory of an attractive young girl has a place in David's mind alongside a remarkably tactile memory: "I crept close to my mother's side, according to my old custom, broken now a long time, and sat with my arms embracing her waist, and my little red cheek on her shoulder, and once more felt her beautiful hair drooping over me—like an angel's wing as I used to think, I recollect—and was very happy indeed" (VIII). There is less of a mother-son relationship here than of a relationship between a young man and his beloved.

Sexual rivalry, in fact, is partly responsible for David's disliking his mother's suitor, Mr. Murdstone. "I was jealous that his hand should touch my mother's in touching me," David says at one point (II). And again:

> "Let us say 'good night,' my fine boy," said the gentleman, when he had bent his head—*I* saw him!—over my mother's little glove.
>
> "Good night!" said I.
>
> "Come! Let us be the best friends in the world!" said the gentleman, laughing. "Shake hands!"
>
> My right hand was in my mother's left, so I gave him the other. "Why, that's the wrong hand, Davy!" laughed the gentleman.
>
> My mother drew my right hand forward, but I was resolved, for my former reason, not to give it to him, and I did not. I gave him the other, and he shook it heartily, and said I was a brave fellow, and went away. (II)

After Mr. Murdstone marries Mrs. Copperfield, one of the first things David discovers is, "My dear old bedroom was changed, and I was to lie a long way off" (III). As the jilted man, David is understandably stand-offish: "He seemed to be very fond of my mother—I am afraid I liked him none the better for that" (IV). But David is also completely loyal to his love, and never more so than when he learns his mother has died in childbirth:

> From the moment of my knowing of the death of my mother, the idea of her as she had been of late had vanished from me. I remembered her, from that instant, only as the young mother of my earliest impressions, who had been used to wind her bright curls round and round her finger, and to dance with me at twilight in the parlour. What Peggotty had told me now, was so far from bringing me back to the

> later period, that it rooted the earlier image in my mind. It may be curious, but it is true. In her death she winged her way back to her calm untroubled youth, and cancelled all the rest.
>
> The mother who lay in the grave, was the mother of my infancy; the little creature in her arms, was myself, as I had once been, hushed for ever on her bosom. (IX)

The projected death wish is at once self-pitying and a sentimental yearning for an ultimate consummation of love, to die with a loved one wrapped in her arms.

In effect, Clara Copperfield never really does die, for she lives in David's memory and in the resurrected being of herself called Dora Spenlow. David falls in love with his mother all over again when he falls in love with Dora. Mrs. Copperfield is as well described by the following remarks as is the younger, future Mrs. Copperfield: "Dora seemed by one consent to be regarded like a pretty toy or plaything" (XLI). "The cookery-book made Dora's head ache, and the figures made her cry" (XLI). Like Clara Copperfield, Dora is youthful in appearance, knows nothing about keeping house, cries a good deal, and is excessively vain, especially about her curls. The reader recalls Clara's remark about being a "childish widow" and a "childish mother" when Dora has this conversation with David:

> "Will you call me a name I want you to call me?" inquired Dora, without moving.
>
> "What is it?" I asked with a smile.
>
> "It's a stupid name," she said, shaking her curls for a moment. "Child-wife." (XLIV)

Their marriage actually secures the identification between David's mother and his bride, for Betsey Trotwood says, "I think of poor dear Baby this morning" (XLIII), and Peggotty tells David "she saw my own dear mother married."

One critic has written that David marries Dora because, having lost his mother, he needs "to replace what he has lost by an identical substitute."[8] Another critic says, "Childishness gives an innocent cast to [Dora's] coquetry; it serves to disguise, dilute, or repress the sexual nature of her appeal, and it is precisely this kind of repression which characterizes an oedipal attraction—which makes it seem acceptable, that is, to the son who seeks his mother in his sweetheart."[9] Since David's marriage to Dora is motivated in part by his sexual interest in his mother, the proper word for this discussion, of course, is incest. Neither David nor the Victorian reader could allow himself to think of such a tabooed subject in connection with the events of *David Copperfield,* and thus the incest motif in the novel went unnoticed in the nineteenth century.

For this same reason, the Victorian conviction that a Dickens novel would not deal with a subject as forbidden as incest, there has been until recently no public recognition of the incest motif in the widely read novel, *Hard Times* (1854). But Tom Gradgrind and his sister Louisa have always interested readers, not all of whom may have been as sure of themselves as was F. R. Leavis in *The Great Tradition*: "The psychology of Louisa's development and of her brother Tom's is sound. Having no outlet for her emotional life except in her love for her brother, she lives for him, and marries Bounderby—under pressure from Tom—for Tom's sake."[10] In a keenly perceptive article entitled, "The Brother-Sister Relationship in *Hard Times,*" Daniel P. Deneau says Dr. Leavis puts the case well, although "he stops short and fails to examine the matter as fully as it deserves."[11] The remarkable thing here is that Deneau puts the case more convincingly than Leavis, and then he himself stops short.

Not once does Deneau mention the words "incest" or "incestuous." The furthest he will go in that direction is to say, "Tom and Louisa experience an abnormal brother-sister relationship." This sentence occurs near the beginning of Deneau's article. After decisively supporting his thesis, he says in his last sentence,

> At first glance, Tom's robbery and Louisa's unsuccessful marriage may seem to be Dickens's sole way of depicting their failures, and in turn the failure of the system and philosophy which moulded them; a closer look, however, makes clear that Dickens uses a more subtle, a more psychological means of asserting the moral dangers of Gradgrindism, namely, an abnormal brother-sister relationship.

The very evidence Deneau uses to reach his conclusion suggests he should have been talking about incest all along.

Sexual feeling between brother and sister in *Hard Times* flows one way, from Louisa to Tom. Furthermore, Tom plays upon Louisa's feeling for him: he tells her, "I hate everybody except you" (I, viii); he tries to persuade her to marry Bounderby for his sake by physically "encircling her waist with his arm" and drawing her "coaxingly to him" and "he pressed her in his arm, and kissed her cheek" (I, xiv). If Louisa marries Bounderby, Tom says, "We might be so much oftener together—mightn't we? Always together, almost—mightn't we?" (I, xiv). There are any number of passages in the novel which demonstrate Louisa's more than sisterly affection for her brother, but none is quite so effective in showing incestuous longing as the following lines from a bedroom scene. Tom's short, evasive replies to Louisa are omitted.

> Long after Louisa had undressed and lain down, she watched and waited for her brother's coming home. That could hardly be, she knew, until an hour past midnight; but in the country silence, which did anything but calm the trouble of her thoughts, time lagged wearily. . . .
>
> She waited yet some quarter of an hour, as she judged.

> Then she arose, put on a loose robe, and went out of her room in the dark, and up the staircase to her brother's room. His door being shut, she softly opened it and spoke to him, approaching his bed with a noiseless step.
>
> She kneeled down beside it, passed her arm over his neck, and drew his face to hers. . . .
>
> "Tom, have you anything to tell me? If ever you loved me in your life, and have anything concealed from every one besides, tell it to me." . . .
>
> "My dear brother:" she laid her head down on his pillow, and her hair flowed over him as if she would hide him from every one but herself: "is there nothing that you have to tell me? Is there nothing you can tell me if you will? You can tell me nothing that will change me. O Tom, tell me the truth!" . . .
>
> "As you lie here alone, my dear, in the melancholy night, so you must lie somewhere one night, when even I, if I am living then, shall have left you. As I am here beside you, barefoot, unclothed, undistinguishable in darkness, so must I lie through all the night of my decay, until I am dust. In the name of that time, Tom, tell me the truth now!" . . .
>
> "You may be certain;" in the energy of her love she took him to her bosom as if he were a child; "that I will not reproach you. You may be certain that I will be compassionate and true to you. You may be certain that I will save you at whatever cost. O Tom, have you nothing to tell me? Whisper very softly. Say only 'yes,' and I shall understand you!"
>
> She turned her ears to his lips, but he remained doggedly silent. . . .
>
> "You are tired," she whispered presently, more in her usual way. (II, viii)

This long quotation shows explicitly that Louisa is sexually involved with her brother; her sexual feeling for Tom is, in fact, presented more clearly than the sexual flow between any other sibling pair in Dickens, including Tom and Mary Pinch, John and Harriet Carker, and Paul and Florence Dombey. It is not necessary for Deneau to be as hesitant as he is: "Dickens's reference to 'a loose robe' and Louisa's more pointed reference to her state of undress—' "barefoot, unclothed" '—are pretty insistent details. I suggest . . . that sexual overtones hover over the scene, or, more plainly, that the scene has the atmosphere of a seduction." The scene does indeed have the atmosphere of a seduction, an incestuous seduction, and this is the perversion Mr. Gradgrind unknowingly refers to when he says, "There are qualities in Louisa, which—which have been harshly neglected, and—and a little perverted" (III, iii).

Hard Times is by no means the last Dickens novel to contain sexually abnormal family relationships. If Jenny Wren's sadistic treatment of her father in *Our Mutual Friend* (1865) is not sexually motivated, that motivation is certainly present in Lizzie Hexam's protective actions toward her brother Charley. The critics of *Our Mutual Friend,* moreover, have paid some attention to the sexual connection between Bella Wilfer and her father, Mr. Reginald W. Wilfer. In *The Maturity of Dickens,* Monroe Engel says, "Mr. Wilfer, though he loves Bella, is fully as much her child or her proxy lover as her father."[12] Robert Morse takes a stronger stand in an essay which discusses "doubleness" in *Our Mutual Friend*: "The most grotesque use of doubleness is found in reversals of the natural role: Bella calls her Pa her younger brother, 'with a dear venerable chubbiness on him'—although much of the time she patronizes him in an unpleasantly arch and incestuous way as if he were a faithful but unimportant lover." Bella's "incestuous way" with her father is immediately relevant to the concerns of the present essay.[13]

Father and daughter find one another mutually attractive, especially with regard to the rest of the Wilfer family. Bella tells her relatives, "I always did love poor dear Pa better than all the rest of you put together, and I always do and I always shall!" (II, viii). Mr. Wilfer would say the same of Bella, who contrasts strongly with Mrs. Wilfer, an unlikable, angular, domineering woman with a touch of frigidity in her make-up. When one kisses Mrs. Wilfer, he finds her cheek "as sympathetic and responsive as the back of the bowl of a spoon" (II, viii). Within doors, Mrs. Wilfer wears gloves most of the time, and she habitually ties a pocket handkerchief about her head. The best Mr. Wilfer can say of her to Bella is, "Your mother has, throughout life, been a companion that any man might—might look up to—and—and commit the sayings of, to memory—and—form himself upon—if he—" (II, viii). Bella, on the other hand, is an enticing young woman.

With brown eyes and brown curls, she is "about nineteen, with an exceedingly pretty figure and face" (I, iv). K. J. Fielding finds her "natural and fresh; the most natural and attractive woman in Dickens's novels, in fact the only one."[14] Angus Wilson says Bella "brings some liveliness and some sexual warmth to Dickens' heroines."[15] Bella's father can personally attest to his daughter's "sexual warmth" for she is continually kissing, hugging, and fondling him. Once when Mr. Wilfer is sitting alone after his wife goes to bed, Bella comes to him in night clothes:

> A light footstep roused him from his meditation, and it was Bella's. Her pretty hair was hanging all about her, and she had tripped down softly, brush in hand, and barefoot, to say good night to him.
>
> "My dear, you most unquestionably *are* a lovely woman," said the cherub, taking up a tress in his hand.
>
> "Look here, sir," said Bella; "when your lovely woman marries, you shall have that piece if you like, and she'll make you a chain of it. Would you prize that remembrance of the dear creature?"
>
> "Yes, my precious." (II, xvi)

Evidence of this kind of rapport between father and daughter is plentiful in the novel.

A chapter entitled, "In which an Innocent Elopement

Occurs," shows Bella buying her father an expensive suit of clothes, taking him to Greenwich for dinner, giving him money, and toying with him as she might toy with an embarrassed lover. "I like to have you all to myself today," Bella says. "I was always your little favorite at home, and you were always mine. We have run away together often, before now; haven't we, Pa?" (II, viii). The outing is for Mr. Wilfer "perhaps the happiest day he had ever known in his life." They dine in a little room overlooking the river while Bella tells her father stories of adventure, stories in which she and Mr. Wilfer are always together. When he momentarily gets out of sorts, "seeing him look grave and downcast, she took him round the neck and kissed him back to cheerfulness again."

Throughout the time Bella is courted by John Rokesmith, her father is either in her thoughts or physically present at her meetings with Rokesmith. He is party to her secret wedding; he shares the wedding dinner; and he has a permanent place in his daughter's new home. When Bella reminds him she is no longer *his* lovely woman, Mr. Wilfer responds, "I am well aware of it, my dear, . . . and I resign you willingly" (IV, iv). Bella says, "Willingly, sir? You ought to be broken-hearted." Mr. Wilfer would have been broken-hearted were he to have lost his daughter, but he knows he will never lose her. Bella tells him, "Now we are a partnership of three, dear Pa."

Our Mutual Friend, Charles Dickens' last completed novel, returns full circle to the earlier novels George Orwell spoke of which had as their ideal endings people living together in an incestuous atmosphere. Bella's incestuous way with her father repeats a motif, an incest motif, which appears over and over again in Dickens' novels; it appears with varying degrees of intensity, as these pages have shown, in *Martin Chuzzlewit, Dombey and Son, David Copperfield, Hard Times,* and *Our Mutual Friend.*

The concern found in Dickens' novels both with orphans and with incest gains significance when it is studied in connection with the subject of sexual repression. Before joining these three topics, however, it is convenient to discuss them separately in order to appreciate fully the meaning and importance each has for the other.

Many readers understand the orphans in Dickens as the novelist's way of rejecting his own parents. For example, Vereen Bell notes there are few satisfactory parent-child relationships anywhere in Dickens' fiction, a conspicuous, explainable element of his art, she says, and "Obviously it reflects the lasting influence of his own childhood."[16] Steven Marcus writes of how Dickens was depressed whenever he thought about his father's neglect of him, so that in all the work subsequent to *Pickwick Papers,* "the image of the delinquent or inadequate parent becomes the very paradigm of wickedness, indeed a primary source for Dickens's inspiration as a novelist."[17] Edgar Johnson sees all of the surrogate parents who move through *David Copperfield* as "dissolutions and refusions of Dickens's own actual parents or of facets of his feelings about them, separated from each other and for the most part not related to David at all, so that without filial disloyalty David may feel toward them in the different ways Dickens did toward his father and mother."[18] Dickens' lasting feeling toward his parents was largely shaped by the best-known incident in his life, when, at the age of twelve, he was taken out of school and away from home to be put to work in a dirty, decaying, rat-infested blacking warehouse. George Ford writes, "At the most crucial stage of a child's development, . . . Dickens believed that he had been wilfully abandoned by his parents. . . . From this well-known incident, then, the specter of insecurity became lodged in Dickens' mind and would never disappear."[19]

Dickens' sense of personal insecurity and parental cruelty may indeed account for his fictional orphans, but there are a good many other reasons for their being in the novels, reasons that have textual rather than biographical validity. The child who is not dependent upon parents, who is alone in the world, is somewhat freer to define himself, to seek his own identity, than is the child bound by family ties. Novels of education, in particular, can focus on individual development without the gratuitous complications of family relationships. The novelist, in effect, has many options freely available to him when he writes about orphans. The isolated child who perforce has his own ego at the center of his existence may grow to be extremely self-reliant or neurotically self-centered. On the other hand, he may come to rely upon society to provide him with institutional parent substitutes, or, more likely in Dickens, society will reject him, thus intensifying both his search for authority and a novel's theme of alienation. The child who needs affection, security, and wisdom dramatically finds himself disinherited, without social roots, without a family past. But such a child can draw upon inner resources and innate qualities of the human spirit to become an uncorrupted adult with a unique capability, the potential to be free in the world. He can give of himself without having prior debts to pay; he can do good in the world without having his motives suspect because of hidden claims upon him; and perhaps above all, the orphan is free to extend himself by embracing the world and loving outwardly. This ability to love outwardly contrasts diametrically in Dickens with the ability for love consequent upon the constrictions of incest.

Whereas there is outward centrifugal movement associated with the development of an orphan theme, incest betokens inward centripetal movement. An incestuous feeling acts in itself as a centripetal force attracting pairs of a family unit. There are psychological, if not physical, cords binding mother and son, father and daughter, or brother and sister. The incestuous relationship is sheltered and essentially regressive, always inwardly retreating to primal family associations. Incest also prompts one to retreat from adult responsibilities and realities, thus fostering an inordinate dependence upon parents or other family members. The individual remains conserving rather than revolutionary, immature rather than completely developed, because he lessens his possibilities for enlargement and growth by intensifying a family connection he would commonly break in the course of normal development. While the orphan has a chance to grow as he welcomes new experience, the person with incestuous longings will stunt his growth as he narrows experience to his immediate family. And here again is the contrast between loving outwardly and loving inwardly. The subject of incest has as much thematic potential as the subject of orphans.

Some readers, however, prefer to see biographical implications behind the incest theme in Dickens' novels. Jack Lindsay and Mark Spilka work with the idea that in real life Dickens was incestuously attracted to his sister Fanny and also to his sister-in-law Mary Hogarth. Mary became for Dickens a substitute "for the lost love of his youth, his own sister Fanny" and numerous heroines in Dickens become in turn substitutes for Mary. Here is Spilka on the story of this attraction:

> Mary had lived with Dickens and his wife during the first year of their marriage. She was sixteen at the time, demure, pretty, and, in Dickens' eyes, angelic; her hero-worship intoxicated the young writer, who considered her "the chief solace of his labours," and clearly preferred her to his wife. When she dies in his arms, after a sudden illness, he slipped a ring from her finger and wore it till his death. For years he longed for burial beside her; he also dreamed of her re-

> peatedly, and called her memory an essential part of his being, as inseparable as his heartbeat.[20]

Since Mary was herself a surrogate for Fanny Dickens, Spilka concludes, "Dickens' feelings toward Mary Hogarth were incestuous; when he enshrined her in idealized heroines like Little Nell and a host of sexless saints, he was trying to disguise those feelings." In one way or another, the incest motifs in his novels are Dickens' unconscious attempts to rid himself of incestuous longings by writing them out of his system.

If this view is credible, there are reasons which are equally believable to explain why, although he wrote about incest, Dickens could not write about normal adult sexuality. One frequently comes across flat statements in critical literature such as George Orwell's remark, "Sexual love is almost outside [Dickens'] scope,"[21] or Mario Praz's comment, "In sexual relationships, the novelist Dickens is the champion of the strictest orthodoxy."[22] But here again Mark Spilka is an articulate Freudian: he argues that Dickens was evasive in depicting love because he repressed romantic feeling after Maria Beadnell, a banker's daughter, rejected his amorous, intense pursuit of her when he was seventeen years old, deeply in love, and without financial prospects. Spilka emphasizes the repressive element in Dickens:

> If we can assume, for a moment, that such vigorous repression was already part of Dickens' makeup when he met Maria Beadnell, then it helps to explain his excessive delight in her childish ways; it also explains his sudden longing for the same delights, some twenty-five years after their first affair, when he received a letter from his former sweetheart. At their second meeting, however, the coyness of the stout, middle-aged matron seemed grotesque; Dickens was severely jolted, and aware of his own folly in expecting something else. He was understandably blind, however, to that powerful emotional arrest which explains his folly: that same

> arrest which apparently led him to marry a childish and incompetent woman; which made him turn for support to her younger sisters (whose sexual innocence seems obvious); and which finally led him to pursue a nineteen-year-old girl, Ellen Ternan . . . .[23]

The reader who is uncomfortable with criticism that draws parallels between fiction and biography will nevertheless find in the fifteen novels Dickens wrote a predilection for sexless love between normal adult lovers and an avoidance of adult sexual feeling.

The dynamics of sexual repression help to explain why a Dickens novel contains an extraordinary number of orphans, incestuous situations, and hardly any insights into normal adult sexuality. The "powerful emotional arrest" Spilka wrote about with relation to Dickens' partiality for childish women is, from another point of view, a force which accounts for repressed sexuality in Dickens' novels. One has only to recall the psychological nature of repression to understand why the act of restraining sexual expression is a dynamic act, and why it relates with telling significance to Dickens' fictional concern with orphans and incest.

Sexual repression, like any other kind of repression, is an attempt to control energy which by its very nature seeks release. The stronger the restraints, the stronger the blocks to release, the more insistently will repressed energy seek expressive outlets. Charles Dickens himself worked with the dynamics of repression in the character of Bradley Headstone in *Our Mutual Friend*: Headstone speaks of himself as a man who lives by "repressing himself daily" (II, vi), and Dickens shows the aftermath of such repression in a symbolic scene between Headstone and Rogue Riderhood.

> He [Headstone] dropped into a chair, and laughed. Immediately afterwards, a great spirt of blood burst from his nose.

> "How does that happen?" asked Riderhood.
>
> "I don't know. I can't keep it back. It has happened twice —three times—four times—I don't know how many times—since last night. I taste it, smell it, see it, it chokes me, and then it breaks out like this." (IV, i)

The ability of whatever is repressed to escape its bonds in one form or another is a phenomenon which Taylor Stoehr has recently applied to an analysis of *Bleak House*:

> Society, whose systematizing, delimiting, law-making aspects are represented by Tulkinghorn and the legal profession, enchains and represses human nature, which nevertheless expresses itself in violation of these laws (the crossing of class boundaries, the breaking of sexual mores) ; the result is illegitimacy, guilt, and the need for deception and hypocrisy; finally the deception must be uncovered, the illegitimacy punished, the guilt expiated; and all this is accomplished when the repression—originally a cause of the crime, now a part of the guilt and the attempt to hide it—becomes so constrictive that the system itself splits open in an explosion of violence, representing both a return to nature and impulse and also a punishment and atonement for the sin.[24]

Repression, then, is operative with regard to individuals, as Dickens put the case in *Our Mutual Friend,* and it is operative with regard to the abstraction "human nature," as Stoehr put the case in his analysis of *Bleak House*. It is also dynamically operative in still another way.

Dickens' work gives an abundance of testimony to the likelihood that the novelist repressed his ability to write about normal adult sexuality. The broad middleground of sexual feeling and experience is absent in Dickens. On the other hand, he writes almost obsessively about two extremes of love, the inward-looking, intense sexuality connected with his incest theme, and the outward-looking, enlarging kind of love which is consequent upon his orphan theme. It is as though pressure from repressing the center of a sexual spectrum forced a flow of sexual expression toward both extremes of the spectrum. In a

Dickens novel, then, orphans and incest are topical outlets for repressed sexuality.

The implications of this conclusion are manifold, not only as they apply to Dickens' work, but as they apply on another level to Victorian society as well. In an age where sexual repression is a family way of life, children who traditionally would have found sexual education within their family unit as preparation for their finding sex outside of the family find instead that they are caught in a tense situation: either the family has been too encompassing and protective, keeping them sexually narrow, or it has abnegated responsibility for sexual education by giving no guidance at all. These extremes in Dickens are represented by the centripetal experiences of incest opposed by the centrifugal experiences of his orphans. One force turns a man inward, and the other force turns him outward. This tension in a Dickens novel or in Victorian society is precipitated, at least in part, by the psychological pressures of sexual repression.

7

Charlotte Brontë's *Villette*

Three of Charlotte Brontë's four novels acknowledge the universal truth that a single person in normal good fortune must be in want of a mate. In *The Professor,* Frances Evans Henri marries William Crimsworth, and they have a son named Victor. *Jane Eyre* finds the heroine married to Edward Rochester, and they too have a son. In *Shirley,* Caroline Helstone marries Robert Moore; Shirley Keeldar marries his brother, Louis Moore. Each of these novels has a conventionally happy ending, and in each novel the Brontë heroine finds sexual fulfillment in marriage. Charlotte Brontë's last novel, *Villette,* ends differently. The heroine Lucy Snowe finds bliss not with marriage, conjugal love, and children: she finds bliss living alone, reading love letters, and waiting for a man she has never even kissed. "M. Emanuel was away three years. Reader, they were the three happiest years of my life" (Chapter XLII).

A fact unacknowledged by critics of *Villette* is that Lucy Snowe is a sexually frigid young woman who learns to come to terms with her abnormal sexuality during the course of the novel. At the end of *Villette,* Lucy is happy, healthy, and emotionally secure. During most of the novel, however, she suffers from nervous and mental disorders; she is frequently depressed, physically ill, and emotionally distraught. In medical terms, she is brought to health by a psychoanalytic catharsis: painful emotional desires she had repressed, sexual desires, libidinal desires, are released in a curative experience. Lucy's catharsis is the purgation of her repressed desires. That purgation takes the form of a sexual experience which readers of *Villette* have not heretofore recognized, but which fashions the climax of the novel and is a turning point in Lucy's life.

What every reader of *Villette* does recognize is Lucy's tendency to live as passively as possible and to repress as many emotions as possible. "I liked peace so well," Lucy says, "and sought stimulus so little, that when the latter came I almost felt it a disturbance, and wished rather it had still held aloof" (I). If a stimulus or disturbance does not hold aloof, then we are shown early in the novel that Lucy will nevertheless try to retain her composure. As a young girl, presumably an orphan, Lucy leaves the kinsfolk with whom she stays to visit her godmother, Mrs. Bretton, who lives with an only son, John Graham Bretton. Soon after Lucy's arrival, Mrs. Bretton hears of a friend's death and agrees to care for a six-year-old girl named Pauline (Polly) Home while the widower Mr. Home travels for health. At the leave-taking between father and daughter, Mr. Home sobbed, Polly held up quivering lips, Mrs. Bretton shed a tear or two, and the narrator stayed aloof: "I, Lucy Snowe, was calm" (II).

Polly eventually develops a crush on John Graham Bretton, who is sixteen, and when she is told it is time to rejoin her father on the continent, she cries. Lucy wonders, "How will Polly get through this world, or battle with this life? How will she bear the shocks and repulses, the humiliations and desolations, which books, and my own reason tell me are prepared for all flesh" (III). As a teenager, Lucy confronts life armed with books and her reason. When she leaves the Brettons, she goes to care for a rheumatic cripple, Miss Marchmont, who is Lucy's sole companion until Miss Marchmont dies. Lucy is now nearly twenty-three. She eventually decides to leave England and sets out for Villette, the capital city of Labassecour. With a new life ahead, she feels emotional stirrings, but once again the disturbance is kept in check.

> The sky . . . was monotonously gray; the atmosphere was stagnant and humid; yet amidst all these deadening influences, my fancy budded fresh and my heart basked in sunshine. These feelings, however, were well kept in check by the secret but ceaseless consciousness of anxiety lying in wait on enjoyment, like a tiger crouched in a jungle. The breathing of that beast of prey was in my ear always; his fierce heart panted close against mine; he never stirred in his lair but I felt him: I knew he waited only for sun-down to bound ravenous from his ambush. (VII)

Rather than suffer the "consciousness of anxiety" which metaphorically lies in wait on enjoyment, Lucy suppresses the joyful feelings that would arouse the beast.

Once in Villette, Lucy finds employment with Madame Beck, first as nursery-governess to her three children and then as an English teacher in her school for young women. The little dormitories in Madame Beck's establishment had long ago been nuns' cells. These surroundings fit Lucy Snowe, for she leads a cloistered existence. Her knowledge of life in general and of love in particular is mostly secondhand.

In England, she looked on at Polly's childish infatuation for John Graham Bretton, and she heard Miss Marchmont tell of a great, unfulfilled love over which she pined for thirty years. In Villette, she observes the coquetry of a seventeen-year-old flirt, Ginevra Fanshawe. Miss Fanshawe toys with the same John Graham Bretton whom Polly and Lucy knew in England, but the boy has now become a practicing doctor in Villette. Miss Fanshawe's response to the thought of a serious romance is lighthearted: *"Vive les joies et les plaisirs! A bas les grandes passions et les sévères vertus!"* (IX) Ginevra Fanshawe prefers the foppish Colonel Alfred de Hamal to her grave, deep-feeling, thoughtful young physician.

Since Lucy is in the confidence of both Ginevra and Dr. John, she becomes a party to their affair. She listens to Dr. John speak of Ginevra's being fair and good; he speaks of her charms, her sweetness, and her innocence. On the other hand, she hears Ginevra constantly mock her lover. She also pays attention to Ginevra when the coquette scornfully turns on her:

> I suppose you are nobody's daughter, since you took care of little children when you first came to Villette: you have no relations; you can't call yourself young at twenty-three; you have no attractive accomplishments—no beauty. As to admirers, you hardly know what they are; you can't even talk on the subject: you sit dumb when the other teachers quote their conquests. I believe you never were in love, and never will be; you don't know the feeling: and so much the better, for though you might have your own heart broken, no living heart will you ever break. Isn't it all true? (XIV)

Lucy answers honestly, "A good deal of it is true as gospel, and shrewd besides."

In addition to being third party to an unlucky romance, Lucy looks on at other happenings. She finds a billet-doux meant for someone else; she attends a fête where young people flirt with one another; she acts the part of a gay lover in a school play; she goes to an art museum, a concert, and the theatre. At the museum, a picture of Cleopatra interests her. The fleshly queen, done in the manner of Peter Paul Rubens, lay half-reclined on a couch. Lucy thinks, "She had no business to lounge away the noon on a sofa. She ought likewise to have worn decent garments; a gown covering her properly, which was not the case" (XIX). At the theater, Lucy responds less critically and more emotionally to a performance by the great actress Vashti:

> The strong magnetism of genius drew my heart out of its wonted orbit; the sunflower turned from the south to a fierce light, not solar—a rushing, red, cometary light—hot on vision and to sensation. I had seen acting before, but never anything like this: never anything which astonished Hope and hushed Desire; which outstripped Impulse and paled Conception; which, instead of merely irritating imagination with the thought of what *might* be done, at the same time fevering the nerves because it was *not* done, disclosed power like a deep, swollen, winter river, thundering in cataract, and bearing the soul, like a leaf, on the steep and stately sweep of its descent. (XXIII)

Lucy shows us that she can get emotionally involved in a performance. She has desires which need to be hushed; she has nerves which can become fevered. This buried self in Lucy's being does not behave as we have come to expect Lucy to behave. Given life, this self would not boast, "I, Lucy Snowe, was calm."

There is more than one dimension to the character of Lucy Snowe. The secondhand life she leads relates meaningfully to the nature of her own inner life; her repressed emotions, her repressed sexuality, define her as tellingly as outward characteristics. But her repressed life is hard to get at because she narrates what she wants to narrate and hides what she wants to hide, or must hide in response to psychic demands. However, there are ways to recognize and determine Lucy's inner life so as to make it accessible to analysis. The careful study of her language is one very obvious entry to her essential being.

Everything Lucy says must not be taken as literal or factual truth. We are told, "I, Lucy Snowe, plead guiltless of that curse, an overheated and discursive imagination" (II), but we know too that Lucy is subject to dreamlike, insensible behavior. Once she tells us, "Harassed, exhausted, I lay in a half-trance" (VI), and another time she says, "In catalepsy and a dead trance, I studiously held the quick of my nature" (XII). Somewhere between these extremes of sensibility, between the overly rational and the overly bewildered, stands Lucy Snowe. Guiltless of an overheated and discursive imagination, though, she is not. On the packet-ship named *The Vivid,* which takes her from England to Labassecoeur, Lucy says,

> In my reverie, methought I saw the continent of Europe, like a wide dream-land, far away. Sunshine lay on it, making the long coast one line of gold; tiniest tracery of clustered town and snow-gleaming tower, of woods deep-massed, of heights serrated, of smooth pasturage and veiny stream, embossed the metal-bright prospect. For background, spread a sky, solemn and dark-blue, and—grand with imperial promise, soft with tints of enchantment—strode from north to south a God-bent bow, an arch of hope.
>
> Cancel the whole of that, if you please, reader—or rather let it stand, and draw thence a moral—an alliterative, text-hand copy—
>
> "Day-dreams are delusions of the demon." (VI)

This description of Europe objectifies an inner fantasy, a longing for a fairyland world of serenity and peace that contrasts with the real world Lucy knows. Reality for Lucy is a tense struggle born of her need to suppress an emotional part of her nature.

The calm she yearns for is interestingly played against a storm scene in Villette. The scene emphasizes Lucy's struggle to suppress powerful desires that disturb her. To a Freudian critic, these desires are expressions of libidinal hunger, and there are sexual overtones to her description of lightning bolts which split and pierce. "I well remember whatever could excite," Lucy says. "Certain accidents of the weather, for instance, were almost dreaded by me, because they woke the being I was always lulling, and stirred up a craving cry I could not satisfy" (XII). One night the being wakes to a thunder-storm whereby Lucy's craving is felt intensely:

> The tempest took hold of me with tyranny: I was roughly roused and obliged to live. I got up and dressed myself, and creeping outside the casement close by my bed, sat on its ledge, with my feet on the roof of a lower adjoining building. It was wet, it was wild, it was pitch-dark. . . . I could not go in: too resistless was the delight of staying with the wild hour, black and full of thunder, pealing out such an ode as language never delivered to man—too terribly glorious, the spectacle of clouds, split and pierced by white and blinding bolts. (XII)

This emotional, excitable person wages war with the prim Lucy Snowe. At times, the struggle is sharply defined.

Once at twilight the implse of a "wild longing" is subdued by being "softened into a wish with which Reason could cope" (XV). The regulated, equable, quiet life which Reason approves opposes "the natural character, the strong native bent of the heart" which Feeling approves (XVII). Lucy asks, "But if I feel, may I *never* express?" The answer comes immediately: " 'Never!' declared Reason" (XXI). Reason is stern and demanding, and yet, "We shall and must break bounds at intervals, despite the terrible revenge that awaits our return" (XXI). The battle within Lucy is fought by "the dry, stinting check of Reason" against "the full, liberal impulse of Feeling" (XXIII).

The character in *Villette* who best understands this battle is Professor Paul Emanuel, the one person in the novel who probes the depths of Lucy Snowe. He tells her, "You remind me, then, of a young she [sic] wild creature, new caught, untamed, viewing with a mixture of fire and fear the first entrance of the breaker-in" (XXI). In a psychological sense, Paul Emanuel is himself this "breaker-in." He has a peculiar relationship with Lucy from the first moment he meets her.

A small, dark, spare man in spectacles, M. Paul has skill in physiognomy. Madame Beck asks her cousin to use that skill in reading Lucy's countenance, and we learn for the first time what we are later shown over and over again, that Paul intends to see through Lucy. "The little man fixed on me his spectacles. A resolute compression of the lips, and gathering of the brow, seemed to say that he meant to see through me, and that a veil would be no veil for him" (VII) . When she knows Paul better, Lucy makes a point of commenting on his talent for "compelling" people (XX) . Although she wants to avoid him, she is constrained to behave differently:

> I could not, however, be true to myself. Yielding to some influence, mesmeric or otherwise—an influence unwelcome, displeasing, but effective—I again glanced round to see if M. Paul was gone. No, there he stood on the same spot, looking still, but with a changed eye; he had penetrated my thought and read my wish to shun him. (XX)

This compelling man with an ambiguously mesmeric power Lucy calls the "vague arbiter of my destiny" (VII) .

Paul's power to see through Lucy is kept before us by Lucy's extraordinary awareness of Paul's eyes. With both slighting references and serious concern, she constantly talks about his eyes. She speaks in passing of "his thorough glance" (XIV) and then stands rooted as "two eyes first vaguely struck upon, and then hungrily dived into me" (XIV) . His glances were "fed with sharp shafts," and when Paul asks Lucy to act in a school play, these shafts pierce her reserve:

> A thousand objections rushed into my mind. The foreign language, the limited time, the public display. . . . Inclination recoiled, Ability faltered, Self-respect (that "vile quality") trembled. *"Non, non, non!"* said all these, but looking

> up at M. Paul, and seeing in his vexed, fiery, and searching eye a sort of appeal behind all its menace—my lips dropped the word *"oui."* (XIV)

After the play, Paul asks Lucy to be his partner at a ball. She tells him she does not dance. " 'For once I must,' was the answer; and if I had not slipped aside and kept out of his way, he would have compelled me to this second performance."

Once as Lucy sits in the refectory musing about life, she looks up to see how "two eyes filled a pane of that window; the fixed gaze of those two eyes hit right against my own glance: they were watching me" (XXI). Paul's behavior was not unusual: "It was very much his habit to wear eyes before, behind, and on each side of him." When Lucy displeases him, "Monsieur curled his lip, gave me a vicious glance of the eye, and strode to his estrade" (XXI). Lucy remembers "that blue, yet lurid, flash out of his angry eye" (XXVI); there is no surprise by his stepping up one morning and whispering solemnly that he "had his eye on me."

Despite Paul's compelling, mesmeric eye, he is no hypnotist, no mesmerist. His ability to pierce the veil of Lucy's composure is, for the reader, simply another entry to Lucy's inner life. Paul shows that Lucy can respond to a man without consciously wanting to respond. When Paul's searching eyes penetrate Lucy's subconscious mind, the complexity of her being is once again revealed. Lucy Snowe has psychological depth. Her unwilling reactions to Paul's commands must be thought of in connection with the craving cry she cannot satisfy, the being she cannot lull, the wild longing she tries to suppress—these are all elements of psychological significance. The reader of *Villette* becomes intensely interested in watching the complete unfolding, the complete arousal, of Lucy's buried self.

Paul Emanuel helps to demonstrate the possibility of Lucy's responding from within, and is even the eventual hero, or anti-hero, to this novel's heroine; but the person who fully arouses Lucy's repressed sexuality is Dr. John Graham Bretton. Subconsciously, Lucy is sexually attracted to Dr. John early in the novel. She meets him when she first arrives in Villette, although, unbelievably, she does not recognize him as her godmother's son: "I saw that he was a young, distinguished, and handsome man; he might be a lord, for anything I knew: nature had made him good enough for a prince, I thought. His face was very pleasant; he looked high but not arrogant, manly but not overbearing" (VII). To Lucy, "There was goodness in his countenance, and honour in his bright eyes." She follows him as he directs her to an inn. "I could not see my guide; I could only follow his tread. Not the least fear had I: I believe I would have followed that frank tread, through continual night, to the world's end."

Lucy and Dr. John meet several times at Madame Beck's house, where Lucy is employed and Dr. John attends the sick when he is not flirting with some mysterious young woman. Characteristically passive and neutral in outward appearance, Lucy is inwardly very upset over these flirtations. When she mistakenly identifies the portresse, Rosine Matou, as the object of Dr. John's affections, there are signs about Lucy which point toward sexual jealousy. She describes Rosine as "an unprincipled though pretty little French grisette, airy, fickle, dressy, vain, and mercenary" (XI). Lucy pretends she is mystified by Rosine's attraction for Dr. John:

> But Rosine! My bewilderment there surpasses description. I embraced five opportunities of passing her cabinet that day, with a view to contemplating her charms, and finding out the secret of their influence. She was pretty, young, and wore a well-made dress. All very good points, and, I suppose,

> amply sufficient to account, in any philosophic mind, for any amount of agony and distraction in a young man like Dr. John. Still, I could not help forming half a wish that the said doctor were my brother; or at least that he had a sister or a mother who would kindly sermonize him.

If Lucy had a sense of humor, she would laugh at herself for passing Rosine's apartment five times in order to look her over. If she were or could be honest with herself, she would recognize her own sexual jealousy of Rosine. Lucy consciously forms half a wish that Dr. John were her brother; she subconsciously forms the other half to the wish that Dr. John were her lover.

Nothing Dr. John does, says, or gives to Lucy in subsequent months indicates he is sexually interested in her. They become better acquainted; they even renew the easy family relationship they had in England when Lucy lived in the Bretton household. Lucy willingly admits to admiring Dr. John, but she is unable to admit the extent of her sexual desire for him. After years of repressing her sexual emotions, however, Lucy can no longer hold those emotions in check. She is in somewhat the same position as an unmarried young woman who has passed the normal age of bethothal and who is terrified lest she lose and lest she should not lose her virginity in time to come. Given Lucy's character, an outright sexual experience is out of the question. But psychologically, she comes as close as she possibly can to having that experience.

It begins when she dreams of a letter from Dr. John and then actually sees the letter she dreamed about in Rosine's hand. "A letter! The shape of a letter similar to that had haunted my brain in its very core for seven days past. . . . Strong magnetism drew me to that letter now" (XXI). Just as Paul had once compelled her to act against her will, now the letter magnetically draws her. She overacts to the letter tremendously, perhaps neurotically. "I knew it, I felt it to be the letter of my hope, the fruition of my wish, the release from my doubt, the ransom from my terror." All of this, and she hasn't even opened the envelope: "I held in my hand not a slight note, but an envelope, which must, at least, contain a sheet: it felt, not flimsy, but firm, substantial, satisfying." This foreplay continues. "I held in my hand a morsel of real solid joy: not a dream, not an image of the brain, not one of those shadowy chances imagination pictures. . . ." The reader can hardly endure three pages of this kind of thing.

Finally, Lucy puts the unopened envelope away: "Having feasted my eyes with one more look, and approached the seal, with mixture of awe and shame and delight, to my lips—I folded the untasted treasure, yet all fair and inviolate, in silver paper, committed it to the case, shut up box and drawer, reclosed, relocked the dormitory, and returned to class." The erotic handling of the letter magnifies it beyond all proportion to what it is worth merely as a piece of paper. The exaggerated care taken in hiding it supports the idea that the letter is being treated as a sexual object with attendant sexual guilt. In its envelope, folded, wrapped in silver paper, the letter is placed in a case, shut in a box, put in a drawer, and enclosed within a room that stands within a locked dormitory.

The circumstance of Lucy's actually reading the letter finds a parallel in a woman experiencing sexual intercourse. Bent on finding solitude, Lucy takes a key, mounts three staircases in succession and reaches a dark, narrow, silent landing which leads to a deep, black, cold garret. Certain that no one would follow her, no one would interrupt, she shuts, and presumably locks, the garret-door.

> I took my letter, trembling with sweet impatience; I broke its seal.
>
> "Will it be long—will it be short?" thought I, passing my hand across my eyes to dissipate the silvery dimness of a

> suave, south wind shower.
>
> It was long.
>
> "Will it be cool?—will it be kind?"
>
> It was kind.
>
> To my checked, bridled, disciplined expectation, it seemed very kind; to my longing and famished thought it seemed, perhaps, kinder than it was.
>
> So little had I hoped, so much had I feared; there was a fullness of delight in this taste of fruition—such, perhaps, as many a human being passes through life without ever knowing. (XXII)

The transformation of Dr. John's good-natured, chatty letter to a sexually stimulating love object momentarily causes Lucy to project emotional feelings to Dr. John himself. He meant, Lucy says, "not merely to content *me*—but to gratify *himself*. A gratification he might never more desire, never more seek—an hypothesis in every point of view approaching the certain; but *that* concerned the future. This present moment had no pain, no blot, no want; full, pure, perfect, it deeply blessed me." The satisfaction lasts just a moment, because something as strange as Lucy's imagined intercourse happens next.

Unsettled by the excitement of her experience, and constitutionally a nervous person, Lucy sees the spectral black-and-white figure of a nun. Legend has it that the nun, supposedly long dead, was the victim of an unhappy love affair. Why Lucy sees the nun at precisely this moment is open to speculation. Perhaps the frame of Lucy's mind and the state of her emotions make the gothic apparition credible at this time. Or Charlotte Brontë might be making fun of Lucy Snowe and the whole gothic tradition in literature: the ghostly nun turns out to be Colonel Alfred de Hamal, a dandified young man, a fop, who comes to Madame Beck's establishment courting the giddy, flirtatious Ginevra Fanshawe. This undermines Lucy's fright and mocks the gothic tradition. But at the moment

Lucy sees the "nun," she is real, not illusory. She is, in fact, just as real to Lucy as her imaginary sexual experience.

The reality of that latter experience is powerfully brought home by a passage which contains Freudian imagery so classic, it might well serve as a textbook example on how to recognize disguised sexual meaning. Three weeks after Lucy's adventure in the garret room, she tells us of a new influence acting upon her life—sadness is held at bay, and she develops a new belief in happiness. The following passage says that the change was sexually brought about:

> Conceive a dell, deep-hollowed in forest secrecy; it lies in dimness and mist: its turf is dank, its herbage pale and humid. A storm or an axe makes a wide gap amongst the oak-trees; the breeze sweeps in; the sun looks down; the sad, cold dell, becomes a deep cup of lustre; high summer pours her blue glory and her golden light out of that beauteous sky, which till now the starved hollow never saw. (XXIII)

If a reader cannot recognize vaginal imagery here, there is little chance he will ever accept a Freudian reading of literature.

Lucy gets four more letters from Dr. John. "When I first tasted their elixir, fresh from the fount so honoured, it seemed juice of a divine vintage: a draught which Hebe might fill, and the very gods approve" (XXIII). And then the letters stop. Lucy realizes that Dr. John has become romantically attached to the girl he once knew as Polly Home, who is now an eighteen-year-old beauty called the Countess Paulina Mary de Bassompierre. She has all of his attention. The river which flowed from Dr. John to fertilize the arid part of Lucy's life was bending to another course: "It was leaving my little hut and field forlorn and sand-dry, pouring its wealth of waters far away" (XXVI).

A symbolic burial of the life-giving letters finally ends the affair.

Lucy takes the letters in a sealed jar to the foot of an old pear tree. The timber of the tree was sound, "only there was a hole, or rather a deep hollow, near his root. I knew there was such a hollow, hidden partly by ivy and creepers growing thick round; and there I meditated hiding my treasure" (XXVI). Just as Lucy proved herself to be sexually suitable for Dr. John, there is a symbolic replay of that suitability here: "I cleared away the ivy, and found the hole; it was large enough to receive the jar, and I thrust it deep in." With the jar containing the letters thrust deeply within the secret hole, Lucy re-enacts her sexual experience with Dr. John before she inters it for good. The exaggerated burial shows she has done with part of her life forever. She goes to a tool shed: "I fetched thence a slate and some mortar, put the slate on the hollow, secured it with cement, covered the whole with black mould, and, finally, replaced the ivy. This done, I rested, leaning against the tree; lingering, like any other mourner, beside a newly-sodded grave."

Something more than five letters has been buried. Lucy has at long last purged herself of repressed sexual desires; furthermore, she will have no future desire for sexual experience. The imaginary intercourse she experienced in the garret while reading Dr. John's letters was in effect a psychoanalytic catharsis. Once torn by Reason and Emotion, by fear of sex and desire for sex—torn, in short, by an outer self struggling with an inner self, she has now laid the ghost of her sexual passions. She no longer needs to respond to love as a normal woman with normal desires. In fact, Lucy now slowly begins to accept herself for what she naturally is, and here is a climax of *Villette* and a turning point in Lucy's life.

What Lucy naturally is, of course, is what Charlotte

Brontë made her—a sexually unattractive, highly strung, frigid woman past her youth. In a letter to the publisher George Smith, Charlotte Brontë wrote,

> Lucy must not marry Dr. John; he is far too youthful, handsome, bright-spirited, and sweet-tempered; he is a 'curled darling' of Nature and of Fortune, and must draw a prize in life's lottery. His wife must be young, rich, pretty; he must be made very happy indeed. If Lucy marries anybody, it must be the Professor—a man in whom there is much to forgive, much to 'put up with.' [1]

The movement of the plot takes Dr. John to the young, rich, pretty, Paulina de Bassompierre. The direction of Lucy's life changes too. She moves away from her fantasied romance with Dr. John to a realistic acceptance of Professor Paul Emanuel. Whereas Lucy could not be more wrong for John Bretton, she could not be more right for Paul Emanuel. Neither youthful, handsome, bright-spirited, nor sweet-tempered, and certainly not a "'curled darling' of Nature and of Fortune," Paul Emanuel, in his forties, makes a fitting sexual mate for Lucy Snowe.

Their connection is better described as asexual rather than sexual. Making the two mutally accept a sibling relationship has the effect of helping to desex both of them as they draw together. "He asked whether, if I were his sister, I should always be content to stay with a brother such as he. I said, I believed I should; and I felt it" (XXXIII). Paul calls Lucy *"Petite soeur,"* but he needs to be assured that she understands his meaning. "A close friend I mean—intimate and real—kindred in all but blood? Will Miss Lucy be the sister of a very poor, fettered, burdened, encumbered man?" (XXXV). To this parody of a romantic proposal, Lucy gives assent:

> "Is monsieur quite serious? Does he really think he needs me, and can take an interest in me as a sister?"

"Surely, surely," said he; "a lonely man like me, who has no sister, must be but too glad to find in some woman's heart a sister's pure affection."

"And dare I rely on monsieur's regard? Dare I speak to him when I am so inclined?"

"My little sister must make her own experiments," said he; "I will give no promises. She must tease and try her wayward brother till she has drilled him into what she wishes." (XXXV)

Since Paul's proposal makes no sexual claims on her, Lucy is delighted to accept it: "I envied no girl her lover, no bride her bridegroom, no wife her husband; I was content with this my voluntary, self-offering friend." Significantly, Lucy compares her relations with Paul to relations she would feel to have undesirable romantic overtones, those of girl and lover, bride and bridegroom, wife and husband. For Lucy, Paul is sexually safe.

He has even sworn himself to celibacy: "I was willing to be his sister, on condition that he did not invite me to fill that relation to some future wife of his; and tacitly vowed as he was to celibacy, of this dilemma there seemed little danger" (XXXVI). For added insurance, Madame Beck has told Lucy that Paul intends to die a virgin (XXXIV). He once loved a girl named Justine Marie, but their marriage was prevented, the girl became a nun, and she died in the flush of youth. When Paul meets her again in heaven, he wants to be as chaste as she was when she died. There is ample evidence here that Charlotte Brontë has deprived Paul of all sexual potential, and yet there is more on this point.

Paul tells Lucy in his own words that he has buried all passion in his life:

Don't suppose that I wish you to have a passion for me, Mademoiselle; Dieu vous en garde! What do you start for? Because I said passion? Well, I say it again. There is such a word, and there is such a thing—though not within these

> walls, thank Heaven! You are no child that one should speak of what exists; but I only uttered the word—the thing, I assure you, is alien to my whole life and views. It died in the past—in the present it lies buried—its grave is deep-dug, well-heaved, and many winters old. (XXIX)

The burial imagery is significant, for it parallels the figurative language Lucy used when she buried Dr. John's letters and that part of her being which was capable of a passionate response to love. In denying passion, Paul and Lucy are two of a kind. The reader of *Villette* hears sexual as well as religious overtones when Paul lovingly calls Lucy, "My little English Puritan" (XLII).

At the close of the novel, Paul finally does propose marriage to Lucy: "Lucy, take my love. One day share my life. Be my dearest, first on earth" (LXI). He then leaves Labassecour on business which takes him across the Atlantic for three years. "Reader," Lucy says, "they were the three happiest years of my life" (XLII). When the time comes for Paul's return, a storm racks the Atlantic, and it is left to the reader's imagination whether or not he ever does return.

Since very few people are able to sustain interest in the plot of *Villette,* one hardly cares if Paul comes back. *Villette* draws its strength from the character Lucy Snowe, and this is somewhat ironic, for Charlotte Brontë disliked her heroine. "I am not leniently disposed towards Miss *Frost,*" she wrote George Smith. "From the beginning, I never meant to appoint her lines in pleasant places." In another letter, she wrote,

> As to the name of the heroine, I can hardly express what subtlety of thought made me decide upon giving her a cold name; but, at first, I called her 'Lucy Snowe' (spelt with an 'e'); which Snowe I afterwards changed to 'Frost.' Subsequently, I rather regretted the change, and wished it 'Snowe' again. . . . A *cold* name she must have; partly, perhaps, on

> the *'lucus a non lucendo'* principle—partly on that of the 'fitness of things,' for she has about her an external coldness.[2]

The descriptive phrase, "an external coldness," is less meaningful than the adjective "frigid," and it is the adjective which better suits Lucy Snowe.

As a psychological study of sexual frigidity, *Villette* is a remarkable book. Charlotte Brontë anticipated Freud and his followers by more than half a century, for her handling of Lucy's problem is thoroughly modern. She takes a woman who constitutionally needs to repress her sexual emotions, and who finds that those emotions cannot be successfully repressed. An imagined sexual experience serves as a catharsis which induces the discharge of repressed libidinal energies. Once Lucy has purged herself of sexual desire, she is free to accept a man who has the same sexual proclivities she has. As a fictional character, Lucy may indeed make an unattractive heroine; as a psychological study in frigidity, she is fascinating.

8

George Meredith's *The Ordeal of Richard Feverel*

In an enjoyable and highly readable biography entitled *The Ordeal of George Meredith,* Lionel Stevenson makes a disquieting statement about Meredith's best-known novel: he says, *"The Ordeal of Richard Feverel* had been reviewed sparsely and unperceptively."[1] That the book was "reviewed sparsely" is debatable, for when the novel first appeared in 1859, it was reviewed immediately by *The Leader, The Critic, The Saturday Review, The Athenaeum, The Spectator, The Illustrated London News, The Westminster Review, Bell's Weekly Messenger, The Morning Chronicle, Thacker's Overland News,* and *The Daily News.* But there is no question that the book was reviewed "unperceptively." George Meredith wrote a letter to Mr. Samuel Lucas saying that no one had perceived the main design and moral purpose of his book, and on October 14, 1859, Lucas drew upon Meredith's letter for a review of *Richard Feverel* in *The Times.* By means of Lucas' two-column review, Meredith spoke publicly about his own novel. And yet the question of how to read Meredith perceptively was still to be answered. When L. T. Hergenhan recently surveyed all of the reviews mentioned above for his article "The Reception of George Meredith's Early Novels," he wrote, "Without exception, reviewers failed to realize that *Richard Feverel* is primarily 'a history of father and son,' as the subtitle suggests."[2]

Today everyone acknowledges *Richard Feverel* as a history of father and son, and critics agree with Meredith about the main design and moral purpose of his book: the novel shows that no system of education can succeed if the originator of the system conceives it out of a personal passion. Sir Austin Feverel satisfies a personal passion as he educates his son, and his system must therefore fail because of the foundation upon which it is placed. But although this is clear to modern readers, there are other problems which remain. John W. Morris wrote, "Throughout the body of Meredithian criticism many valid comments on *Richard Feverel* are to be found; but because they are fragmentary and largely unsystematic, the essential question of the novel's status as a work of literary art has been left unanswered."[3] C. L. Cline reviewed the entire state of Meredith scholarship and concluded, "Biographers and historical scholars would seem to have done most of their work with Meredith. Though new facts will surely continue to be discovered, they will be predictably minor in importance. What has not been done extensively is to re-examine Meredith's novels in the light of contemporary standards of criticism."[4] After more than one hundred years of commentary, the call has gone out for academic spadework on *Richard Feverel.*

A contemporary approach which will help to get the project under way is to study *Richard Feverel* with the aid of basic psychological precepts. Psychological criticism has not yet turned extensively and persuasively to problems of esthetic evaluation, to answering, for example, the question of a novel's status as a work of art; it is preeminently suited, however, to focus on patterns of behavior displayed by figures in literature in order to call attention to a novelist's ability to handle psychological truths. This contributes in the long run to esthetic evaluation if for no other reason than because it helps one to understand why characters behave as they do, and understanding must precede responsible judgment. In *Richard Feverel,* George Meredith has grasped a psychological truth about sexual repression and he presents this truth in such a way that it informs the entire novel. Psychological criticism in this case helps to explain the behavior of the hero Richard Feverel and to outline the artistic structure of his novel.

At the base of the structure are events associated with Richard's birth. His father is Sir Austin Feverel, Baronet, of Raynham Abbey; his mother is an adulteress who runs off with a poet just after Richard's birth. Thus, after five years of marriage Sir Austin is left with loneliness, a boy in a cradle, and an enormous amount of bitterness. "He forgave the man: he put him aside as poor for his wrath. The woman he could not forgive. She had sinned everyway. . . . She had blackened the world's fair aspect for him" (p. 19).[5] His only solace from the affair is his son, whom he intends to rear by a system predicated on his own unhappy experiences with people. One of the two primary concerns of the System is with pride: "My son possesses Pride, say. Human Pride is a well-adjusted mixture of Good and Evil. Well; it tempts him to conceive that he is more than his fellows. Let it, as it can, lift him to *be* more than his fellows, and at once he will cease to conceive it: the fight will have been fought: the Devil will be dead" (p. 11). The other concern of the System is with sin, the handmaid of malevolent women: "Sin is an alien element in our blood. 'Tis the Apple-Disease with which Nature has striven since Adam" (p. 11). Sir Austin never spells out exactly what he means by the "Apple-Disease," but he uses the term to call to mind a blend of sin, sex, and women. Here, for example, is the way he thinks of a father's solemn responsibility toward his son: "By hedging round the Youth from corruptness, and at the same time promoting his animal health, by helping him to grow, as he would, like a Tree of Eden; by advancing him to a certain moral fortitude ere the Apple-Disease was spontaneously developed, there would be seen something approaching to a perfect Man" (p. 12).

Behind the rhetoric lies the fact that Lady Feverel's desertion motivated her husband to protect himself from ever again being hurt by the action of another human being, particularly by a woman. Sir Austin's System is designed to protect him from enduring further pain as much as it is designed to make his son approach some dimly eyed ideal of human perfectibility. In practice, the System attempts to keep Richard hedged around from sexual corruptness, even from sexual experience whether innocent or corrupt. Through Richard, Sir Austin wages war and for a time wreaks his revenge on the sexual urge itself. He wants his son to repress physical and psychic sex drives, and as the unquestioned head of Raynham Abbey he carefully suppresses whatever in his opinion betokens sexuality.

The System has its effect. By the time Richard is in his teens, a young friend, Ripton Thompson, "thought one or two things in his leader rather odd: for instance, his proficiency in manly sports and excercises, joined to his habit of calling his father, Papa, and not Governor, and his entire ignorance about the ways of the girls, and indifference to them" (p. 37). People at Raynham are put on their guard against displaying any visible symptoms of sexual passion. "No gadding about in couples," decreed the Baronet. "No kissing in public. Such occurrences no boy should witness" (p. 133). A by-product of these strictures is Richard's prudishness concerning his own body. Before his seventh birthday Richard resists a complete medical examination; before his fourteenth birthday he refuses to strip for such an examination. Sir Austin is puzzled:

> "A boy who has no voice but mine, Doctor," he said; "Whose spirit is clear to me as day—he enters another Circle of nature, and I require to be assured of his bodily well-being, and this boy, educated in the seclusion of a girl, refuses—nay, swears he will not." (p. 38)

The doctor tells Sir Austin that Richard refuses to strip because he is no longer a child, but Sir Austin does not understand that by keeping Richard ignorant of sex he is thoroughly confusing the boy about all things even remotely sexual, including the propriety of a medical examination.

Sir Austin has tunnel vision when it comes to sex. "You know my opinion, Doctor: we are pretty secure from the Serpent till Eve sides with him" (p. 39). The Baronet is almost monomaniacal on the subject. "Dr. Clifford could not help thinking there were other temptations than that one of Eve. For youths and for men, Sir Austin told him. She was the main bait: the sole to be dreaded for a youth of good pure blood: the main to resist" (p. 40). When Richard's cousin, Clare Doria, becomes of marriageable age, Sir Austin tells Mrs. Doria that his niece's presence is no longer desirable at Raynham, for Clare has become potential bait to be resisted. The girl has in fact fallen in love with Richard, but Sir Austin need not have worried. "Love of that kind, Richard took for tribute. He was indifferent to Clare's soft eyes. The parting kiss he gave her was ready and cold as his father could desire" (p. 136). That Richard takes Clare's love as tribute testifies to the success of the System in inculcating pride within the boy; that he is indifferent to Clare's sexual charm testifies to still another success of the System. Sir Austin is delighted with Richard's behavior and promises him yachts and horses; he grows eloquent toward his son in laudation of manly pursuits.

There is a reason why *The Ordeal of Richard Feverel* insists on Richard's manly pursuits, on his proficiency in sports and exercises, on his abilities as a rider and as a swimmer. The novel demonstrates a truth about the psychology of sexual behavior with particular regard to repression: put simply, the axiom which is illustrated says that if sexual drives are repressed, then the energy generated by the repressed drives must in some way be dissipated. Physical activity dissipates that energy and throughout puberty and adolescence Richard is physically active. Mental activity can also dissipate repressed sexual energy, and the novel makes much of Richard's activity as a poet. He writes bundles upon bundles of poetry until the day his father discovers the manuscripts and has his son pitch them into the flames. "No Feverel has ever written Poetry" (p. 131). And there is yet another effort in *Richard Feverel* to deal with the psychology of sexual repression—the novel attempts to show what happens to an eighteen-year-old boy awakening to natural physiological urges when sexual outlets are peremptorily closed. In delicate and masterful prose, Chapter Seventeen, "An Attraction," shows Richard relieving sexually caused tensions by the age-old expedient of masturbation.

The scene opens with Richard in bed. "All night Richard tossed on his bed with his heart in a rapid canter, and his brain bestriding it, traversing the rich untasted world, and the great Realm of Mystery, from which he was now restrained no longer." Sexually of age, he dreams of girls, and of romantic figures in a medieval setting:

> His heart was a lightning steed, and bore him on and on over limitless regions bathed in superhuman beauty and strangeness, where cavaliers and ladies leaned whispering

> upon close green swards, and knights and ladies cast a splendour upon savage forests, and tilts and tourneys were held in golden Courts lit to a glorious day by ladies' eyes, one pair of which, dimly visioned, constantly distinguishable, followed him through the boskage and dwelt upon him in the press, beaming while he bent above a hand glittering white and fragrant as the frosted blossom of a May-night. Awhile the heart would pause and flutter to a shock: he was in the act of consummating all earthly bliss by pressing his lips to the small white hand. Only to do that, and die!

Richard is thrilled by thought of the kiss. "He was intoxicated by anticipation. For that he was born. There was, then, some end in existence, something to live for! to kiss a woman's hand, and die!" Sexual excitement wakes him; he leaps from the couch and rushes to pen and paper "to relieve his swarming sensations by writing poetry." Now George Meredith uses the psychologically relevant term when he says, "Sir Austin had shut that safety-valve." Sir Austin had forbidden his son to write poetry. In frustration, Richard is sent "panting to his outstretched length and another headlong career through the rosy-girdled land."

A little before five o'clock in the morning "the madness of the fever abated somewhat" and Richard walks out into the air. "Sir Austin had slept no more than his son. Beholding him so early abroad, his worst fears were awakened." He goes to Richard's room to find the couch "a picture of tempest." Chairs are upset, drawers left open, slippers thrown about. "The abashed Baronet dared not whisper to his soul what had thus distracted the youth." But the signs are so unmistakable that Sir Austin says to himself, "Not an hour must be lost in betrothing Richard, and holding him bond to virtue." While Sir Austin now recognizes his son's sexual need and resolves to find a wife for him, Richard is on his way to the boat house by the riverside where he will shortly take care of his own sexual need by masturbating.

On one level of action Richard is shown rowing a boat; he dissipates his sexual energy through physical activity. On another level, cloaked by rowing imagery, he is shown abusing himself:

> Strong pulling is an excellent medical remedy for certain classes of fever. Richard took to it instinctively. The clear fresh water, burnished with sunrise, sparkled against his arrowy prow: the soft deep shadows curled smiling away from his gliding keel. Overhead solitary morning unfolded itself, from blossom to bud, from bud to flower; still delicious changes of light and colour, to whose influences he was heedless as he shot under willows and aspens, and across sheets of river-reaches, pure mirrors to the upper glory, himself the sole tenant of the stream.

After the "shot" of ejaculation Richard feels relieved. "He had pulled through his first feverish energy." Some time passes and he "lapsed into that musing quietude which follows strenuous exercise."

But suddenly Richard is interrupted by a call from a young man named Ralph Morton, who desires to talk with him. Ralph drags Richard "from his water-dreams" and begins a conversation about girls. Ralph, too, has sexually come of age.

> By degrees he [Richard] perceived that Ralph was quite changed. Instead of the lusty boisterous boy, his rival in manly sciences, who spoke straightforwardly and acted up to his speech, here was an abashed and blush-persecuted youth, who sued piteously for a friendly ear wherein to pour the one idea possessing him.

Like Richard, Ralph was "on the frontiers of the Realm of Mystery"; that is, he had become conscious of sex. He talks as a lovesick adolescent of "the wonderful beauty and depth of meaning in feminine names" and Richard finds that he himself is delighted with the subject. "The theme appeared novel and delicious, fitting to the season and the hour." After eighteen years of repressing sex,

Richard discovers an initial delight in forms of sexual expression.

When Ralph leaves, Richard takes pleasure in thinking of the only girl he knows.

> For the first time it struck him that his cousin Clare was a very charming creature: he remembered the look of her eyes, and especially the last reproachful glance she gave him at parting. . . . Why, Clare was the name he liked best: nay, he loved it. Doria, too: she shared his own name with him. Away went his heart, not at a canter now, at a gallop, as one who sights the quarry. He felt too weak to pull.

With the release of sexual libido, Richard takes the thought of Clare as a love object, but "When Nature has made us ripe for Love it seldom occurs that the Fates are behindhand in furnishing a Temple for the flame." The thought of Clare is quickly replaced by the reality of "a daughter of Earth." This chapter on sexual awakening closes as Richard meets Lucy Desborough in an idyllic situation reminiscent of an encounter in the Garden of Eden.

Lucy is out early that morning gathering dewberries on a river island. "A boat slipped towards her, containing a dreamy youth, and still she plucked the fruit, and ate, and mused." Surrounded by green meadows and wildflowers, "she was a bit of lovely human life in a fair setting: a terrible attraction." Richard sees her and "dared not dip a scull." As he floats by unheeded, "Stiller and stiller grew Nature." When he finally lands on the island, Meredith draws upon Shakespeare and Genesis: "Radiant Miranda! Prince Ferdinand is at your feet. Or is it Adam . . . ? The youth looked on her with as glowing an eye. It was the First Woman to him" (p. 150). In a marvelous chapter which contains the true ring of romantic prose, Richard and Lucy fall in love. As the river current takes Richard's boat downstream, "His old life was whirled away with it, dead, drowned. His new life was with her, alive, divine" (p. 155).

Sir Austin meanwhile has set out in search of a proper wife for Richard. The right girl must not only be found, she must also be trained to a position befitting the wife of a Feverel. The mother of such a person turns out to be Mrs. Caroline Grandison, who has eight unmarried daughters all brought up, like Richard, by the rules of a system. Marriage to a Feverel would answer Mrs. Grandison's fondest hopes, and thus she and Sir Austin get along famously. "Together they quashed the Wild-Oats special plea. Mrs. Caroline gave him a clearer idea of his system than he had ever had before. She ran ahead of his thoughts like nimble fire. She appeared to have forethought them all, and taken a leap beyond" (p. 188). Although neither one of them talks specifically about sex or their belief in sexual repression, Mrs. Grandison has done Sir Austin one better in providing the opportunity for her children to release sexual energy by means of physical activity. The girls have a gymnasium in their country home and another gymnasium in their town home. They exercise once a day without intermission on swing-poles, stride-poles, "and newly invented instruments for bringing out special virtues" (p. 191). A professor of gymnastics comes twice a week to superintend. All of this impresses Sir Austin, and especially is he impressed with the thirteen-year-old Carola Grandison. With perhaps seven years of training, she might make a proper wife for his son. Sir Austin and Mrs. Grandison sit in a drawing room, where "they exchanged Systems anew, as a preparatory Betrothal of the Objects of the Systems" (p. 192).

With Sir Austin in London, Richard is free at Raynham Abbey to carry on his courtship of Lucy Desborough, who lives with her uncle on a nearby farm. Richard and Lucy write letters to one another during the day, and meet secretly every night. When the letters and meetings are discovered by a butler named Benson and Sir Austin's nephew, Adrian Harley, the Baronet is immediately informed and Richard is ordered to London to meet Carola Grandison. At first he refuses to leave the country; next, when he does meet his father in the city, Richard does not tell him of his deep love for Lucy. A wedge of sex is used ever more forcefully to widen the relationship between father and son. Although Sir Austin succeeds in having Richard meet Carola, the young man finds the girl delightful not because she is competition to Lucy but because she is a thoroughgoing tomboy. Carola wants to be a boy, wants to ride her pony strideways, and wants to be called Carl. When she asks if she is good-looking, "Richard complimented her by saying, he thought she would grow to be a very handsome chap" (p. 231). But notwithstanding the fact that "A girl so like a boy was quite his ideal of a girl" (p. 233), Richard's heart is with Lucy.

His residence, however, is with his father. Sir Austin keeps a close eye on Richard and manages to have Lucy's uncle send her away to school. For nearly a year Sir Austin and his followers at Raynham Abbey arrange to keep Richard and Lucy apart. But circumstance plays into Richard's hand, and with the help of his old friend, Ripton Thompson, Richard at long last gets together again with Lucy. She is lodged in London with a ripe and wholesome landlady named Mrs. Elizabeth Berry, who becomes party to a secret marriage.

It is Mrs. Berry's wedding ring that symbolically unites Richard and Lucy. At the altar, Richard discovers he has lost the ring he meant to give Lucy, and at the last moment he takes the landlady's ring. Once when Mrs. Berry had told how her husband ran off with another woman nine months after their marriage, she also said, "Here's my Ring. A pretty ornament! What do it mean? I'm for tearin' it off my finger a dozen times in the day. It's a symbol? I call it a tomfoolery for the dead-alive to wear it, that's a widow and not a widow, and haven't got a name for what she is in any Dixonary" (p. 323). The ring foretokens marital unhappiness for Lucy, and it foretokens sexual unhappiness as well. Here George Meredith uses a simile that draws an image of traditional phallic significance: he says of Lucy,

> Omens are against her: she holds an ever-present dreadful one on that fatal fourth finger of hers, that has coiled itself round her dream of delight, and takes her in its clutch like a horrid Serpent. And yet she must love it. She dares not part from it. She must love and hug it, and feed on its strange honey, and all the bliss it gives her casts all the deeper shadow on what is to come. (p. 345)

The penis image suggested by the Serpent is indeed bizarre, and yet in the context of the novel taken whole, it is entirely appropriate.

Sir Austin refuses to accept his daughter-in-law and he will not forgive his son. Richard has said, "If my father loves me, he will love her. And if he loves me, he'll forgive my acting against his wishes" (p. 305). But Sir Austin is too proud and too hurt to forgive. "Richard was no longer the Richard of his creation: his pride and his joy: but simply a human being with the rest" (p. 388). The Devil says to him, "Only be quiet: do nothing: resolutely do nothing: your object now is to keep a brave face to the world, so that all may know you superior to this human nature that has deceived you. For it is the shameless Deception, not the Marriage, that has wounded you" (p. 390). Sir Austin takes the Devil into his bosom, crumples a letter from his son, and tosses it into the fire.

Richard waits anxiously for his father to reply to that

letter. While honeymooning on the Isle of Wight, he tells Lucy almost daily that Sir Austin will write or even surprise them with a visit. The days go by, however, and Richard falls in with a fast crowd headed by Lord Mountfalcon, who becomes more and more interested in Lucy. Lacking worldly sophistication and still sexually naïve, Richard trusts Mountfalcon with his wife. "For the first time in his life [Richard] tasted what it was to have free intercourse with his fellow-creatures of both sexes. The son of a System was, therefore, launched; not only through the surf, but in deep waters" (p. 401). The deep waters begin engulfing Richard when he leaves Lucy on the island so that he may go alone to London in order to make himself more available to a visit from his father.

In London, Richard again finds himself freer than he had ever been at Raynham Abbey. And once again the System backfires. After years of living in sexual ignorance and being required to repress all sexual longings, Richard is now driven by curiosity about sex. Every night for one month he walks the streets after ten o'clock in search of prostitutes. He merely looks at them, rolls his eyes, groans, and talks about regenerating fallen women. Although he is a youth "open to the insane promptings of hot blood" (p. 459), Richard never sleeps with the prostitutes, and yet night after night he is drawn to them, ostensibly with the thought of regenerating fallen women. (The scene in small illustrates a duality in Victorian life—the Victorians were fascinated by illicit sex at the same time they professed to be repelled by it.)

A more dangerous threat to Richard's virtue is the person of Mrs. Bella Mount. When Richard asks, "Who's Mrs. Mount?" he is told, "A sister to Miss Random, my dear boy" (p. 440). Miss Random, a Victorian catchword for loose women, had been introduced earlier in the novel when Sir Austin caught young Ripton Thompson reading a pornographic book in his father's law office. The title page of the book "set forth in attractive characters beside a coloured frontis-piece, which embodied the promise displayed there, the entrancing Adventures of Miss Random, a strange young lady" (p. 169). Lawyer Thompson exclaims, "One of the very worst books of that abominable class!" and he asks Sir Austin if Richard will be allowed to receive his son in the future. " 'Certainly!' the Baronet replied. . . . 'When there is no longer danger of contamination to my son, he will be welcome as he was before. He is a schoolboy. I knew it—I expected it. The results of your principle, Thompson!' " Unlike Richard, Ripton Thompson had not been raised by a System. Ironically, however, whereas Ripton does nothing more than read about Miss Random, Richard is physically seduced by her.

Mrs. Bella Mount is paid by Lord Mountfalcon to keep Richard in London, if necessary by seducing him, while Mountfalcon tries his luck with Lucy on the Isle of Wight. Since Richard needs to satisfy years of a sexually deprived curiosity, she has a relatively easy time of it. They meet first at a dinner party at Richmond where women smoke and pet openly with men who are only interested in sexual flirtations. As days and weeks go by, Richard "began to think that the life lying behind him was the life of a fool. What had he done in it? He had burnt a rick and got married!" (p. 474) The young man seeks amusement; he begins to make late evening calls on Mrs. Mount.

Bella offers Richard a wide variety of sexual entertainment. She tells him stories about women of good repute and pours "a little social sewerage into his ears" (p. 474). One moment she is warmly feminine and the next moment "She was cold as ice, she hated talk about love" (p. 476). Bella Mount is a "wily woman" (p. 479). There is also a touch of perversity about Bella. Richard says, "She's very like a man, only much nicer" (p. 455). Her conversation at times is "man-like" and she loves to masquerade as a man: " 'Ah, Dick! old fellow! how are you?'—arrayed like a cavalier, one arm stuck in her side, her hat jauntily cocked, and a pretty oath on her lips to give reality to the costume. 'What do you think of me? Wasn't it a shame to make a woman of me when I was born to be a man?' " (p. 475). Her favorite role is as a dandy they name Sir Julius, a pose Bella frequently adopts during Richard's evening visits. The narrator asks, "Was ever Hero in this fashion wooed?" (p. 476).

When Richard thinks of his wife Lucy, his mood turns sour. "Charming Sir Julius, always gay, always honest, dispersed his black moods" (p. 478). Bella, clearly a transvestite, keeps Richard fully occupied. Her sexual range is remarkable. Richard tells her, "You saw that I admired you." She answers, "Yes, but a man mustn't admire a man." Though she never expresses an idea, she is unmistakably clever. "She could make evenings pass gaily, and one was not the fellow to the other. She could make you forget she was a woman, and then bring the fact startlingly home to you. She could read men with one quiver of her half-closed eyelashes. She could catch the coming mood in a man, and fit herself to it" (p. 482). In short, Bella Mount is George Meredith's version of Shakespeare's Cleopatra. "She [Bella] understood spontaneously what would be most strange and taking to [Richard] in a woman. Various as the Serpent of old Nile, she acted fallen Beauty, humorous indifference, reckless daring, arrogance in ruin" (p. 483). But whereas Marc Antony was in many respects a match for Cleopatra, Bella plays the game of sex with more enthusiasm than her partner.

At the same time Richard is attracted to Bella for her sinfulness, he wants to reform her. "What can I do for this poor woman?" Richard cries (p. 485). "Poor little thing" is a customary comment he adds when talking about her. "Who cares for you, Bella? I do. What makes my misery now, but to see you there, and know of no way of helping you?" (p. 490). Richard means it when he says, "Oh, Bella! let me save you" (p. 493). Torn as he is with regard to Bella, Richard's other dilemma fitfully plagues him too. His father answers none of his letters, and the thought of Lucy nags his conscience. When he decides to return to Lucy, Bella makes a last play for him. "Far from discouraging him, she said nobly: 'Go—I believe I have kept you. Let us have an evening together, and then go: for good, if you like' " (p. 486). In agreeing to spend that last evening with Bella, Richard makes a fateful decision.

The "Enchantress" receives him with liquor, gaiety, and an occasional revival of Sir Julius. Dispirited, Richard gulps champagne, calls for glass after glass of wine, and wonders, "Was he in Hell, with a lost soul raving to him?" (p. 488) Bella captures his interest by telling how a nobleman first had her when she was sixteen years old, and next she arouses him sexually by appearing in a new guise entirely.

> A white visage reappeared behind a spring of flame. Her black hair was scattered over her shoulders and fell half across her brows. She moved slowly, and came up to him, fastening weird eyes on him, pointing a finger at the region of witches. Sepulchral cadences accompanied the representation. He did not listen, for he was thinking what a deadly charming and exquisitely horrid witch she was. (p. 492)

Beautiful and devilish, Bella enraptures Richard. "Was she a witch verily? There was sorcery in her breath; sorcery in her hair: the ends of it stung him like little snakes." As she dances across the room, Bella laughs at Richard for liking her best disheveled. "He felt giddy; bewitched" (p.

493). And still he thought of saving her, of reforming her. "But in dreaming to save, he was soft to her sin" (p. 496). As Bella kneels at Richard's feet "a devouring jealousy sprang like fire in his breast, and set him rocking with horrid pain" (p. 497). He lifts her, strains her in his arms, and kisses her passionately on the lips.

> She was not acting now as she sidled and slunk her half-averted head with a kind of maiden shame under his arm, sighing heavily, weeping, clinging to him. It was wicked truth. Not a word of Love between them!
>
> Was ever Hero in this fashion won?

Thus ends the chapter entitled "An Enchantress" and with it ends Richard's sexual apprenticeship.

A henchman of Lord Mountfalcon's intercepts a letter Richard has written to Bella; it is worded thus:

> "My beautiful Devil!
>
> "Since we're both devils together, and have found each other out, come to me at once, or I shall be going somewhere in a hurry. Come, my bright Hell-star! I ran away from you, and now I ask you to come to me! You have taught me how devils love, and I can't do without you. Come an hour after you receive this." (p. 500)

Lord Mountfalcon reads the letter, but decides he cannot use it in his pursuit of Lucy because she would first swear it was false and then stick closer than ever to Richard. "I know the sluts," says the Lord. He doesn't know Lucy, however, for while Bella has been seducing Richard, Mountfalcon has had no success in his attempt to seduce Richard's wife.

Mountfalcon's attack on Lucy's virtue is one of two events in Meredith's novel meant to contrast with and emphasize Richard's period of sexual debauchery. Like Bella, Mountfalcon sees the Feverel "victim" almost every evening. Like Richard, Lucy, "the inexperienced wife," sees no harm in the visits. The text itself spells out another parallel:

> Lord Mountfalcon was as well educated as it is the fortune of the run of titled elder sons to be: he could talk and instruct: he was a lord: and he let her understand that he was wicked, very wicked, and that she improved him. The Heroine, in common with the Hero, has her ambition to be of use in the world—to do some good: and the task of reclaiming a bad man is extremely seductive to good women. (p. 499)

But whereas Richard succumbs to Bella, Lord Mountfalcon groans, "I haven't advanced an inch" (p. 500). Unknown to both Richard and Mountfalcon is the fact that Lucy is pregnant. Mrs. Berry finds out that fact when she visits the Isle of Wight, and it is Mrs. Berry who becomes involved in the second event which contrasts with Richard's sexual behavior in London in order to emphasize the nature of his sexual experience.

In London, Bella made love to Richard in the pose of a man, and Richard responded to Sir Julian's advances. Now the scene is played again with the opposite sex: Mrs. Berry, an innocent lesbian, if such there be, makes love to Lucy. Richard's wife hears the news that Sir Austin is ready to receive her and she and Mrs. Berry "chattered on happily till bed-time. Lucy arranged for Mrs. Berry to sleep with her. 'If it's not dreadful to ye, my sweet, sleepin' beside a woman,' said Mrs. Berry" (p. 514). They go upstairs together.

> Then they cooed, and kissed, and undressed by the fire, and knelt at the bedside, with their arms about each other, praying; both praying for the unborn child; and Mrs. Berry pressed Lucy's waist the moment she was about to breathe the petition to Heaven to shield and bless that coming life; and thereat Lucy closed to her, and felt a strong love for her. Then Lucy got into bed first, leaving Berry to put

> out the light, and before she did so, Berry leaned over her, and eyed her roguishly, saying, "I never see ye like this, but I'm half in love with ye myself, you blushin' beauty! Sweet's your eyes, and yer hair do take one so—lyin' back. I'd never forgive my father if he kep me away from ye four-and-twenty hours just. Husband o' that!" Berry pointed at the young wife's loveliness. "Ye look so ripe with kisses, and there they are a-langishin'! . . . You never look so but in bed, ye beauty!—just as it ought to be." Lucy had to pretend to rise to put out the light before Berry would give up her amorous chaste soliloquy. Then they lay in bed, and Mrs. Berry fondled her, . . . and hinted at Lucy's delicious shivers when Richard was again in his rightful place, which she, Bessy Berry, now usurped; and all sorts of amorous sweet things; enough to make one fancy the adage subverted, that stolen fruits are sweetest; she drew such glowing pictures of bliss within the Law, and the limits of the conscience, till at last, worn out, Lucy murmured, "Peepy, dear Berry," and the soft woman gradually ceased her chirp.

Instead of sleeping, Mrs. Berry lay thinking of Lucy, "squeezing the fair sleeper's hand now and then, to ease her love" (p. 515). A barking dog and house noises draw her to the window where she sees a man walking out of the garden into the road. Next morning Mrs. Berry finds a footprint in the garden and some strange guidance has her match it with one of Richard's boots. She tries it from heel to toe a dozen times; the boot perfectly fits the print.

Part of the night, then, Richard stood below a window to the bedroom where his wife lay in bed with Mrs. Berry. To Lucy, the woman was a poor surrogate for her husband. Whereas Richard gave in sexually to Sir Julian, Lucy merely slept beside Mrs. Berry. The respective scenes have played sexual experience and marital infidelity against sexual innocence and marital loyalty. One recalls the omen of the marriage ring Lucy wears: "It's a symbol? I call it a tomfoolery for the dead-alive to wear it, that's a widow and not a widow, and haven't got a name for what she is in any Dixonary" (p. 323).

Richard now feels a strong sense of shame for his infidelity to Lucy and he tries to withdraw from society. He is cool toward his father; he prefers wine to conversation; he says nothing when Sir Austin tells him that he and Lucy are expected at Raynham Abbey. Mrs. Berry brings Lucy to London, but Richard refuses to call on his wife. Sir Austin is told, "Somebody has kissed him, Sir, and the chaste boy can't get over it" (p. 524). This sets Sir Austin thinking "it might be a prudish strain in the young man's mind, due to the System in difficulties." At the moment, Richard has less of a "prudish strain" within him than a goodly amount of severe sexual guilt.

The death of his cousin Clare adds to that guilt. At her deathbed Richard realizes that Clare had always loved him. "The memory of her voice was like a knife at his nerves. His coldness to her started up accusingly: her meekness was bitter blame" (p. 530). Clare's diary shows Richard how his cousin felt about him, as does the fact that Clare dies wearing the lost wedding ring Richard had intended to give Lucy. He tells his aunt, Clare's mother, he is to blame for Clare's death:

> I have killed one. . . . I cannot go with you to my wife, because I am not worthy to touch her hand, and were I to go, I should do *this* to silence my self-contempt. Go you to her, and when she asks of me, say I have a death upon my head that—No! say that I am abroad, seeking for that which shall cleanse me. If I find it I shall come to claim her. If not, God help us all! (p. 535)

Richard goes abroad feeling base and ignoble, thoroughly unworthy of Lucy. "At moments he forgets; he rushes to embrace her; calls her his beloved, and lo, her innocent kiss brings agony of shame to his face" (p. 549). All of the letters sent to him from England are burned unread, and not until an uncle finds him in Germany does Richard learn that Sir Austin has brought Lucy to Raynham Abbey to live there with her new born son. " 'A father!' he kept repeating to himself: 'a child!' And though he knew it not, he was striking the key-notes of Nature. But he did know of a singular harmony that suddenly burst over his whole being" (p. 554). Richard walks alone into a forest. "Something of a religious joy—a strange sacred pleasure—was in him." He picks up a frightened leveret and does not notice the advance warnings of an approaching thunderstorm. The young hare licks his hand and Richard feels thrilled and touched in blood, mind, and heart.

Richard's rebirth continues as the symbolic storm breaks. "Vivid as lightning the Spirit of Life illumined him. He felt in his heart the cry of his child, his darling's touch. With shut eyes he saw them both. They drew him from the depths; they led him a blind and tottering man. And as they led him he had a sense of purification so sweet he shuddered again and again" (p. 558). The baptism in rain water and rebirth in nature purify Richard of sexual grossness, and he becomes a family man. The purification does not completely remake him, however, for he is left with a damning family trait, the Feverel pride.

On his return to Raynham Abbey, Richard stops in London where he receives a letter from Mrs. Bella Mount which tells him how Lord Mountfalcon had used both her and Richard in a complicated plot aimed at Mountfalcon's seducing Lucy. Richard immediately calls upon Mountfalcon to challenge him to a duel. "A mad pleasure in the prospect of wreaking vengeance on the villain who had laid the trap for him, once more blackened his brain" (p. 585). In his haste to fight Mountfalcon, Richard stays with his family only briefly, although Lucy is heartbroken at the thought of his leaving again. He could have forsaken the duel. "But Pride said it was impossible."

The duel is paradoxically meaningless and yet heavily charged with irony: Lucy has never been unfaithful to her husband and Lord Mountfalcon was sexually frustrated; Richard had his pleasure with Bella Mount and both he and Bella regret the affair. Nonetheless, Richard, a dishonorable husband, fights for his wife's honor, which was never lost. Psychologically, Richard fights the duel out of pride and as an act of sexual penance, not as a true affair of honor. But if he desired punishment by death or wound, the novel cheats him. Richard is shot harmlessly in the side, whereas the shock of the duel and Richard's injury derange Lucy. Cerebral fever weakens her and within days she dies. Richard, with the look of a blind man in his eyes, lies silently on his bed—"striving to image her on his brain."

Many causative events precede this tragic ending. At the very beginning of *The Ordeal of Richard Feverel,* however, the novel sets out to investigate the consequences of raising a boy strictly according to the rules of a System. From start to finish everything that happens in the novel relates in some way to a simple query: What happens to a proud youth of high potential when he is denied a sexual education? The answer is equally simple: a young man will somehow manage to acquire sexual knowledge even if doing so precipitates fateful consequences. On the subject of sex, the pages of Meredith's novel have to do with masturbation, phallic symbols, marriage and adultery, nightly prowls in search of prostitutes, pornographic literature, seductions, transvestitism, homosexuality, sexual guilt, and sexual penance. Here is a group of elements which fashion a remarkably modern nineteenth-century novel.

9
Psychologically Oriented Criticism

There are few subjects more hotly debated among people with a professional interest in literature than the business of criticism. Symposia with distinguished participants try in vain to agree on how the critic should explain literature, how he should interpret and evaluate literature. One such symposium found Edmund Wilson, Norman Foerster, John Crowe Ransom, and W. H. Auden each approaching the problems of a critic from a different philosophical position.[1] The so-called Chicago Critics, on the other hand—writers such as Ronald S. Crane, W. R. Keast, Norman Maclean, Richard McKeon, Elder Olson and Bernard Weinberg—adopt roughly the same critical methods.[2] Their methods, of course, differ considerably from the methods of other "schools" of critics. A number of prominent scholars also speak about the business of criticism as proud individualists, if not as defiant eccentrics. Helen Gardner, for instance, searches for the poet's intention in order to find success as a critic: when she feels the intention of the poet with certainty, then she is able to recognize the poem's intention. "If this is to be guilty of 'the intentionalist heresy,' " Miss Gardner says, "I am quite content to be excommunicated for it."[3]

Among the most popular critical approaches to literature in the 1960's is the attempt to place the text of a work of art in its proper context. "The best criticism can hope to do," according to Leslie Fiedler, "is to set the work in as many illuminating contexts as possible: the context of the genre to which it belongs, of the whole body of work of its author, of the life of that author and of his times."[4] Any novel or poem then itself becomes a context of literature, lexical or verbal, which can take its place in the literary environment. Literature influences the way we see literature no less than considerations of sociological, historical, or psychological importance. "The contextual critic," Fiedler says, "desires only to *locate* the work of art, to point toward the place where his contextual circles overlap, the place in which the work exists in all its ambiguity and plenitude."[5]

It is probably impossible for any critic to discuss all of the relevant contexts of literature in a single book. The present writer has made no attempt to do so, nor was it the aim of this book to be exhaustive with regard to any of the manifold concerns of criticism. What the book does attempt is to take limited advantage of extra-literary disciplines in order to frame a small number of novels and poems for a literary examination. If sociology, history, and psychology have provided illuminating contexts for those novels and poems, and if they in turn have suggested literary contexts for critical approaches to other works, then that is the best this book can hope to do.

Sociologists and historians have long been interested in the particular subject of sexual morality in the early and mid-nineteenth century. Their findings are well known: Victorian society at that time was keenly aware of its own moral posture, and society was determined to exhibit the qualities of virtue, goodness, rectitude, and righteousness. Men, women, and children would be self-disciplined; they would conform to the accepted codes of behavior; they would love what is right and eschew what is wrong; in short, they would be good and sexually pure. To ensure their goodness and sexual purity, society threatened nonconformists with legal punishment, economic sanctions, political reprisals, religious penalties, and social ostracism.

In practical terms, Victorian poets and novelists wrote for their age under specific conditions. They obviously acted in accord with or reacted to the demands imposed by the age itself, but the special character of the times made the Victorian era different from the Elizabethan era, let us say, or the twentieth century. The nineteenth-century writer who lived and worked in a society which was self-consciously moral was uniquely influenced by his own upbringing and by his immediate environment. He was raised, for example, to have certain attitudes towards sex and sexual expression, and his novels or poems had to be sold in a marketplace where sexual respectability was defined by censorship laws, watch-dog societies, religious denominations, booksellers, librarians, and the book-buying public. These conditions precluded the kind of sexual expression readers find in Shakespeare's bawdy or in the contemporary works of a Norman Mailer, William Styron, or Allen Ginsberg.

In its attempt to foster goodness and purity, the Victorian age encouraged sexual repression. When sex is repressed, however, human expression is notably affected. Psychologists have a good deal to say on the subject. They say, for example, that when sexuality is dammed up within a person, it will emerge in disguised forms or in ways other than those connected with specifically sexual activities. Since repression operates at unconscious levels in the mind and is therefore silent, observers become aware of psychosexual arrest in an individual when he acts or expresses himself in ways peculiar to given situations. When sexuality should be present and yet is not present, when behavior or language is patently symbolic of sex instead of being forthrightly sexual, then here are signs of repression. Psychologists have discovered dozens of such signs, most of which they have labeled with technical terms. Generally speaking though, no matter how an individual tries to repress his sexual impulses, the sexual energy of those impulses can be discharged through outlets unrecognized by the individual. Furthermore, the evidence of repressed sexuality exists both in life and in literature, and there is striking testimony to that fact in the novels and poems of the Victorian age.

Novelists and poets who wrote in an age notorious for its insistence on repressing sexual expression created works that are remarkably informed with sexuality. These works disguise their sexual content in numerous ways, but the psychologically oriented reader knows how repressed sexuality makes itself manifest, and the literary critic knows how the text of a novel or poem signals the presence of disguised content. With the aid of psychology and a knowledge of literature, one becomes sharply aware of sexuality in Victorian literary art.

Robert Browning's poem, "The Last Ride Together," dramatizes the act of sexual intercourse. Charlotte Brontë's novel, *Villette,* portrays a sexually frigid young woman who paradoxically comes to terms with her frigidity by engaging in therapeutic acts of sex. Various Spasmodic poems, such as Philip James Bailey's *Festus,* Ebenezer Jones's "Emily" and "Zingalee," and Alexander Smith's *A Life-Drama,* deal with sexual desire, masturbation, voyeurism, and sexual perversity. George Meredith's novel, *The Ordeal of Richard Feverel,* has key passages on masturbation, transvestitism, and homosexuality. Alfred Tennyson's idylls, "Lancelot and Elaine" and "Pelleas and Ettarre," have as their controlling images representations of genitalia. At least five of Charles Dickens' novels involve the subject of incest. None of these novels and poems is concerned exclusively with sexual subject matter, but each of them is significantly informed with sexuality.

The quality of sexual expression which is referred to here differs from the well-known surface expressions of sex in Victorian literature. There are flirtatious heroines in Victorian literature—the most notorious is Becky Sharp; there is adultery—the focus of the *Idylls of the King*; there are a seemingly endless number of seductions or attempted seductions. In major works consider James Steerforth and Little Em'ly in *David Copperfield,* James Harthouse and Louisa Gradgrind Bounderby in *Hard Times,* Eugene Wrayburn and Lizzie Hexam in *Our Mutual Friend,* Arthur Donnithorne and Hetty Sorrel in *Adam Bede,* Stephen Guest and Maggie Tulliver in *The Mill on the Floss,* Tito Melema and Tessa in *Romola;* in minor works consider Elizabeth Gaskell's *Ruth;* Elizabeth Barrett Browning's *Aurora Leigh;* Matilda Betham-Edwards' *The White House by the Sea;* Henry G. Jebb's *Out of the Depths.* The Victorian literary portrayal of sexual activity has long been known to have length and breadth, but what the present study of sexual repression and Victorian literature suggests is that nineteenth-century literature portrays the additional dimension of sexual depth.

Fictional characters such as Lucy Snowe and Richard Feverel have mental lives of both conscious and unconscious reality. Their actions are influenced by subliminal sexual motivations, and Charlotte Brontë's *Villette* and George Meredith's *Richard Feverel* show how characters behave sexually in response to those motivations. There is psychological depth to Tennyson's lily maid, Elaine, and to his naïve young lover, Pelleas, and sexual stimuli animate each of these characters. To say that sexuality informs nineteenth-century literature is simply to say that these novels and poems are in touch with the reality of sex in all of its dimensions.

Victorian literature expresses sex in traditional ways by

means of similes, metaphors, symbols—each of which conceals meaning as well as it reveals meaning—and analyzing figures of speech has been of prime importance to the methodology of this book. In its proper context, an act of rowing in *Richard Feverel,* for example, is seen to be symbolic of an act of masturbation. A girl reading a letter in *Villette,* again in context, experiences sexual intercourse on a figurative level. Only rarely have these analyses invoked the technical vocabulary of psychology, as in the essay on "Lancelot and Elaine," where the poem is seen to be structured by the Freudian concept of a fetish. The avoidance of a specialized phraseology, however, does not mean such language is invalid or without value to the literary critic. Norman Holland has recently published a brilliant analysis of Matthew Arnold's "Dover Beach," and Holland does not hesitate to draw upon the vocabulary of Anna Freud's *The Ego and the Mechanisms of Defense.*[6] Depth Psychology has actually been used by literary critics since the first quarter of this century, but many readers still find the technical vocabulary of psychology to be a hindrance rather than an aid to communication.

In his preface to *Mark Twain: The Fate of Humor* (Princeton, N.J., 1966), James Cox wrote that he found Freud's work "indispensable" and the man himself, in terms of evolution, one of the highest developments of the nineteenth-century. But then Cox felt obligated to add, "To have said so much does not mean, I hope, that my study of Mark Twain will be tagged as Freudian, that adjective so conveniently employed faintly to damn and faintly praise." After we have benefited from Freud's influence on literary criticism for half a century, it is unfortunate that critics must still be defensive and apologetic when they adopt a psychological approach to literature. And yet the disclaimers are probably necessary, for to this day many people continue to harbor false notions about the aims and methods of the so-called "Freudian" critics.

Psychological criticism does not claim to displace or supplant all other kinds of criticism. It does not attempt to psychoanalyze novelists and poets by treating their works as clinical data. It does not treat literature as a handmaid to psychology. What it does modestly aim for is acceptance as one of the many limited approaches to literature.

Psychological criticism complements and strengthens other kinds of criticism. For instance, the critic who tries to evaluate a novel or a poem can take profitable advantage of psychology to show the truth or reality of literary behavior by showing how stimuli which motivate a character relate to stimuli which motivate human behavior. This method in turn might establish the unity of a work of art because the actions of major characters frequently structure the works in which they appear. The psychology of sexual repression, for example, explains the behavior of the hero of *Richard Feverel,* and the unity of that novel is defined by the actions of its hero. Here, then, is a specific link between psychological criticism and esthetic or evaluative criticism.

Sections of this book will have special value for particular critical approaches: for biographical criticism there are the inferences suggested by the repressed incest and orphan figures in Dickens' novels; for the New Criticism a recognition of the potential sexuality in metaphor and symbol; for contextualist criticism the revelation of hidden sexuality as a contribution to "ambiguity and plenitude." In the final analysis though, the psychologically oriented critic has exactly the same aims as do all other critics: he wants the fullest possible understanding and the most sensitive appreciation of literature he is able to obtain. These are the ends that must justify any of the means of literary criticism.

Appendix
The Dynamics of Sexual Repression

All men at all times in history live and have lived with sexually repressed desires. That is a truth which psychoanalysis has particularly emphasized since the early writings of Sigmund Freud in the late-nineteenth century. Every adult retains the experience of having passed through not an asexual but a sexual childhood in which mother-son or father-daughter relationships at one time or another involved straightforward sexual desire. The mind energetically represses this desire, but one is left with a lifelong horror of incest. And every adult has experienced as a child the pleasure that comes with genital stimulation, but this experience is also kept in check, though not without leaving one with a sense of guilt, or fear of castration. Sexual repression, then, is familiar to the healthy and the unhealthy, the normal and the abnormal. It is a subject of more than clinical interest, for the effects and manifestations of sexual repression can be studied not only by the psychiatrist who listens to a patient on a couch, but also by the sociologist who watches people on the street, and the literary critic who studies human behavior in the pages of a work of art.

The critic must actually be aware of three broad areas of literary creation which are relevant to findings about sexual repression: repressed thoughts in the unconscious of a writer may find their way into the pages of any given poem or novel; the writer, when reviewing his work, may find he has indeed expressed those thoughts, and then try with total, partial, or no success to suppress them once again; characters created in literature may behave the way they do because of underlying repressions placed in their psyche by an author, or shown to be present by a critic. The fact is, sexual repression is not only normally and universally part of the human condition, but unconscious sexual wishes are constantly driving for expression in order to obtain satisfaction. Neither society nor the individual can tolerate direct and immediate gratification of all sexual impulses, and so defenses are built, which are constantly battered by the sexual energy seeking release, and outlets are found which offer partial or temporary sexual satisfaction. These defenses and outlets are of extraordinary importance to the critic of Victorian literature for once recognized they enable him to deal with a sexual dimension that must be present if art is true to life. People live day by day and function in the real world by repressing sexual impulses they or society cannot allow to have direct expression and immediate gratification; these impulses energetically seek what is denied; and in various ways by various means sexuality is expressed and to a degree satisfied in a manner acceptable to the individual and to society. No less can be said for behavior in literature, and especially Victorian literature, where repressed sexual life had to battle unremittingly for expression. Of critical importance, therefore, is a general knowledge about repression: its definition, its purpose, how it works, and how it is associated with defense mechanisms. Broadly speaking, defense mechanisms identify repression, for they offer recognizable outlets to blocked sexual energies. The entire subject concerns an elementary process and a complex theory that is decidedly Freudian.

There is no clear, unchanging distinction between what is meant by suppression and what is meant by repression. Literary critics and Victorian novelists use the terms as synonyms. For example, in *Martin Chuzzlewit* Charles

Dickens writes of qualities that are released with "all the forced and unnaturally nurtured energy consequent upon their long suppression." In *Our Mutual Friend,* Bradley Headstone is a man who "represses himself" daily. Thus, "wild energy" is kept in till it must burst. Freud writes of suppression in several ways: as an agent of repression, as a synonym for repression, and as a distinctive term. This latter usage of suppression as a distinctive term refers to a conscious resolve not to think of an experience or an idea; for the sake of clarity, these pages will always use the word suppression to mean an act of conscious awareness.

The definition of repression is not as easily handled. In a 1927 essay entitled, "Fetishism," Freud called repression "the oldest word in our psychoanalytic terminology."[1] A year earlier in an "Addenda" to *Inhibitions, Symptoms, and Anxiety* he said,

> In the course of discussing the problem of anxiety I have revived a concept or, to put it more modestly, a term of which I made exclusive use thirty years ago when I first began to study the subject but which I later abandoned. I refer to the term "defensive process". I afterwards replaced it by the word "repression", but the relation between the two remained uncertain. It will be an undoubted advantage, I think, to revert to the old concept of "defence", provided we employ it explicitly as a general designation for all the techniques which the ego makes use of in conflicts which may lead to a neurosis, while we retain the word "repression" for the special method of defence which the line of approach taken by our investigations made us better acquainted with in the first instance.

The Standard Edition of *The Complete Psychological Works of Sigmund Freud* contains an immediate "Appendix" to Freud's "Addenda" which says Freud's account of his usage of repression and defense "is perhaps a little misleading." Repression once described an actual process, and defense described motives for the process. But the concepts were also equated: Freud, in "The Neuro-Psychoses of Defence" (1896), alluded to the "psychical process of 'defence' or 'repression.'" From 1897 onward the word "defence" was used less and less, while the word "repression" began to dominate the writings and was used almost exclusively in the important *Three Essays on the Theory of Sexuality* (1905). After 1905 the predominance of "repression" increased to a point where Freud began speaking of two kinds of repression. Then "defence" as a more inclusive term began appearing, and in 1926 Freud distinguished between the terms in his "Addenda," subsuming one to the other.

Since this lexical history gets more and more difficult to follow with each piece of additional information, there are two practical points to be made here and now: first, it is not feasible to constantly tag a word as Freud used it before and after 1926; second, one might as well take advantage of the fact that the word "repression" has current literary and psychoanalytic usage with reference to a general concept. If there is advantage in thinking of suppression as a conscious resolve to put or keep something out of mind, it is equally advantageous to think of repression as an unconscious resolve to keep certain impulses and drives from entering conscious awareness. Repression always has reference to inner psychic demands. For a useful definition of repression by a scholar of great renown who is professionally considered to be a classical Freudian analyst, there is this formulation by Otto Fenichel: "It consists of an unconsciously purposeful forgetting or not becoming aware of internal impulses or external events which, as a rule, represent possible temptations or punishments for, or mere allusions to, objectionable instinctual demands."[2]

Repression alleviates anxiety, protects one from guilt

feelings, and from feelings of disgust or shame. This is the purposeful aspect of the process. It prevents unbearable internal and external stimuli from prompting the psychic apparatus to vex the conscious mind. Repression excludes from consciousness what one would be aware of as painful and unpleasant. At one extreme, simple forgetting can be evidence of repression; severe threats of pain can actually cause fainting, whereby the conscious mind is protected by a complete cessation of awareness. Since individuals are not uniformly bothered by the same things, there can be no hard and fast rule about what kind of materials need to be repressed *per se*. Social periods have an effect here too. Women in Victorian England were far more likely to repress sexual impulses than women in today's England.

Technically, however, no one can ever repress a sexual impulse. What gets repressed is the idea or group of ideas that are attached to any given instinctual impulse. Instincts are not objects of consciousness; therefore, they cannot be kept out of consciousness. The ideational presentation of an instinct, the so-called instinct presentation, can be kept from conscious awareness. With a characteristic tolerance, Freud addressed himself to this point in an essay entitled, "The Unconscious": "An instinct can never be an object of consciousness—only the idea that represents the instinct. Even in the unconsciousness, moreover, it can only be represented by the idea. If the instinct did not attach itself to an idea or manifest itself as an affective state, we could know nothing about it. Though we do speak of an unconscious or a repressed instinctual impulse, this is a looseness of phraseology which is quite harmless."[3] The precise use of technical terms sometimes gives way to looser popular usage, but in order to fully discuss the complicated subject of repression, one cannot completely avoid a specialized vocabulary.

Many terms of this vocabulary have become familiar to laymen, especially the jargon words associated with the three psychic institutions of id, ego, and superego. The id controls the mind of a newborn child, who reacts chiefly to masses of impulses which lack a guiding consciousness. Soon an ego develops from the id to extend a person's awareness from his own inner world to the outer world in which he functions day by day. Whereas the id shapes the reality of one's inner world, the ego records contacts with external reality, and is descriptively more complex than the id. Part of the ego is conscious (a person "knows" what is here), part is preconscious (materials which can readily be called into consciousness are stored here), and part is unconscious (that is, not readily available to the conscious mind). The particular ego function which is unconscious concerns the operation of the mechanism we are calling repression. This mechanism of the unconscious ego operates at the behest of the superego, itself a growth of the ego. After the id develops an ego, that part of the ego trained by parents and society to form ideals becomes the superego. The superego incorporates parental attitudes, the standards of society, and a person's own ideals for himself. When impulses from the id appear in the ego in pursuit of gratification, the superego passes upon the advisibility of gratification. Each of the three institutions plays a part in repression, and each has a different role to play with different interests to satisfy.

The id is a fountainhead of sexuality called libidinal energy. Libido is psychic energy in the form of sexual hunger, a hunger, unlike food hunger, which will not extinguish the organism if it is not satisfied but will cause severe psychic disturbance if its appetite is not appeased. Libidinous energy exists in the id in a condition of free mobility; the id constantly tries to discharge quantities of this energy. To be successfully discharged, that is, satisfied, libido must be invested in a sexual object. The infant concentrates the libido on himself, a case of primary narcissism that is and always has been a universally shared sexual experience. This condition of ego-libido, of self-love, changes with maturation to object-libido, a process called secondary narcissism. The more libidinous energy invested in an object, the more impoverished the ego, the less "egotistic" the individual. Sexual objects that may be suitably invested with this energy from the id are found by the ego and the superego. But if society provides no sexual object found to be acceptable to the individual's conscience, if the ego and the superego disapprove of a sexual object, then the libidinous energy must be released in substitute objects, or dissipated in dreams and sublimations, or even spent in literature.

Any libidinous energy not directly satisfied by being invested in a sexual object is blocked by a psychic force called resistance. In *A Short Account of Psycho-Analysis* (1923) Freud wrote, "A consideration of the phenomena of resistance led to one of the corner-stones of the psychoanalytic theory of the neuroses—the theory of repression." Resistance is an agent of repression, a force directed against energy emerging from the unconscious. Whereas preconscious memory traits can often be made conscious by a simple act of attention, unconscious phenomena, constantly striving for discharge, are kept in check by this repressing agent, resistance. Conversational silence or an inability to express oneself on a particular topic gives evidence of resistance, as does excessive talking that prevents an accurate understanding of what one says. When what is said differs from what is meant, when a subject triggers an uncalled for antagonism, there is also evidence of resistance, an indication that some feeling, mood, or emotion is seeking expression and being prevented from entering the conscious ego.

The discharges of energy perceived as emotional rather than intellectual stimulants are called affects. An affect is a quantity of excitation with which an idea is charged. The combination of a repressed idea that is linked with an affect is a complex. Under repression, an affect can be separated or detached from the idea with which it normally connects. This severance at times permits an affect to reach consciousness by attaching itself to a substitute idea that is not subject to the block of resistance. Labels seem to proliferate, but the really important point here is that one begins to see how whatever is repressed drives as forcefully as possible to violate the repression and attain expression.

The approaches to motility, the paths into the external world along which excitations must travel in order to be discharged, are controlled by the ego. The ego has the difficult job of trying to control the powerful impulses from the id that demand expression. Freud once wrote that the ego's relation to the id is like a man's relation to a strong horse; the man tries to guide the horse, but at times he must simply guide it where it wants to go if he does not want to be thrown. The simile appears in *The Ego and the Id* (1923) as an extension of these remarks: "The ego seeks to bring the influence of the external world to bear upon the id and its tendencies, and endeavors to substitute the reality principle for the pleasure principle which reigns unrestrictedly in the id. For the ego, perception plays the part which in the id falls to instinct. The ego represents what may be called reason and common sense, in contrast to the id, which contains the passions." The id wants only to satisfy its pleasure-seeking instincts, while the ego must face inward to the demanding id and outward to a world of proprieties, or Victorian restrictions. The id and any civilized society must be at odds, and the ego must somehow reconcile the lawless id with law-abiding society. To bring about this reconciliation, the ego restricts, censors, represses those impulses from the id which would bring about unacceptable social behavior. The ego represses unconscious strivings as a service both to the external world of reality and to the internal world of the superego, where the standards of others develop the ideals of an individual's conscience.

The superego plays a critical role in deciding which instinctual drives from the id will be allowed free and easy entrance to the conscious ego. When the ego complies with the commands of the superego, one feels at rest and secure; when the ego refuses compliance, one feels guilt and remorse. Were it not for the superego and its external counterpart, the conscience of society, the ego would willingly allow an instinct to force itself into consciousness and gain gratification in motility. But the ego represses instinct presentations because it fears the criticism of society and because it fears the criticism of its own superego. Objective anxiety and superego anxiety both motivate repression. Like society, the superego sets up standards according to which sexuality is prohibited and sexual renunciation is demanded. The bounds of the prohibition and the degree of the renunciation depend upon a given society and a given individual, but when excessively strict sexual behavior is demanded, then psychic health is endangered. The ego cannot withstand severe and simultaneous pressures from the external world, the superego, and the id.

A wish or idea aroused in a person which is in sharp conflict with what the person knows and has been taught is socially, ethically, or esthetically acceptable causes pain to the ego. Incompatibility of wish or idea with a person's ego makes an individual try to modify the unacceptable internal demand. In Freudian terms, a neurosis can originate "from the ego's refusing to accept a powerful instinctual impulse in the id or to help it to find a motor outlet, or from the ego's forbidding that impulse the object at which it is aiming." Freud went on to say, in "Neurosis and Psychosis" (1923), that "the ego defends itself against the instinctual impulse by the mechanism of repression. The repressed material struggles against this fate." When sexual wishful impulses of the crudest and most forbidden kind are repressed, the struggle will be extraordinarily fierce. It will be for the ego a source of pain known as instinct anxiety.

Among the ego's motives for repression, then, is the avoidance of three principal types of pain causing anxiety: it seeks to avoid pain caused by objective anxiety, superego anxiety, and instinct anxiety. Anna Freud describes successful repression in *The Ego and the Mechanisms of Defence*: she notes quite simply that successful repression occurs when the ego uses defensive measures to restrict anxiety and pain. The ego-threatening instincts are usually transformed in such a way that they may receive acceptable kinds of gratification, thereby allowing an easy concord among ego, id, and superego.[4] Objective and superego anxiety are restricted when the superego, originally shaped by influences from the external world, does not have to contend with tabooed impulses from the id. Instinctual anxiety, however, can only be restricted when those impulses secure some measure of gratification.

Unless gratified, sexual impulses continually press toward some kind of fulfillment. Their intense force in the form of libidinal energy constantly batters the ego, which must itself constantly spend energy keeping that force in check. The process is dynamic and continuous as long as the repressed libidinal energy cannot leave the unconscious by being granted entrance to consciousness and motility. Libidinous energy is released when pressure from the id overcomes the counterpressure from the ego. Even then there can be no anxiety-free expression of that energy if the superego wants it blocked. And so the ego, to protect itself from conflict, uses a number of defenses which furnish a painless release to libidinous energy. The entire defensive organization of the ego functions unconsciously in fear of the superego while gratifying the id.

The work Freud started on repression and defense was continued by his daughter so successfully that now a classic book on the subject is Anna Freud's *The Ego and the Mechanisms of Defence,* first published in 1937 and in its eighteenth American printing in 1966. Freud wrote of nine defense mechanisms, Anna added another, and in 1937 she wrote about ten different methods the ego used to defend itself in conflicts.[5] Otto Fenichel expanded the list in *The Psychoanalytic Theory of Neurosis* (1945). By 1961 a research team headed by Dr. Grete L. Bibring was able to publish a report in *The Psychoanalytic Study of the Child* on nearly fifty defensive activities of the ego. A "Glossary of Defenses" began, "This glossary is not intended to be a definitive classification of defenses."[6] Although all of the defenses are directed against drives of instinctual significance, there is no sharp distinction among the various forms of defense mechanisms, and no need to deal with them inclusively. Each one of the defenses has the same purpose: to avoid psychic conflict while providing outlets leading to the gratification of internal demands.

Sublimation occurs when instinctual forces with a purely sexual goal are redirected from sexual aims to aims which society holds to be higher. The energy behind an original sexual impulse is released in an area outside the sphere of sexual activity. This defense works when the sublimation has behind it an unchecked stream of libido. Dr. Bibring notes ramifications of the defense:

> Libidinal sublimation involves the inhibition of the manifest sexual aspect and thus the renunciation of direct sexual

> gratification. There are, then, two aspects involved in the complex process of gratification through sublimation: (1) for the sexual drives, a desexualization as far as consciousness is concerned, and (2) the placing of a value judgment: replacing the aim, or aim and object, with something valued by the superego or society.

The sublimation is supported by the instinctual impulse which remains active at an unconscious level. The ego allows the id to express its sexuality in a form acceptable to the superego.

At times instincts which cannot discharge their energy directly do so indirectly by reacting to an actual experience which closely resembles a repressed counterpart and yet sufficiently differs from the repressed so as not to alarm the superego. This is a *déjà vu* defense. One then responds to a situation while feeling that in the past he has already reacted to the same situation. Actually, repressed energy becomes directed to what the defense has made acceptable to the psychic institutions.

A similar defense occurs when a repressed impulse displaces its energy to an associatively connected acceptable impulse and a *derivative* is formed. In other words, the affect of a repressed idea, the quantity of excitation with which the idea is charged, can put its energy at the disposal of a tolerable idea, increase the quantity or even change the quality of the tolerable idea's affect, and thus find free access to consciousness. The derivative is the idea which gains consciousness with an energetically increased or changed affect. When the repressed tries but cannot find an outlet in derivatives, then the ego tends to repress events associatively connected with the originally repressed material. The backfire is called secondary repression. Instead of a derivative escaping the unconscious, the ego represses derivatives as it once repressed original demands. Not all defenses are this complicated.

Denial is a mechanism whereby the ego simply refuses to acknowledge external or internal stimuli which might evoke a painful response. An individual refuses to admit he has seen what he has seen or heard what he has heard. "That person in my dream does not represent my mother" can mean a person feels the figure does represent his mother, but he is able to deny the connection, for to admit it would cause some kind of anxiety, guilt, or shame. Ideas associated with castration and with the loss of love-objects frequently give the ego recourse to denial. In an essay entitled, "Negation" (1925), Freud wrote, "The content of a repressed image or idea can make its way into consciousness, on condition that it is *negated.* Negation is a way of taking cognizance of what is repressed; indeed it is already a lifting of the repression, though not, of course, an acceptance of what is repressed." Thus, unacceptable material can enter consciousness in a negative way, thereby evading psychic condemnation.

Avoidance is a complete turning away from anxiety-fraught situations. Here the ego literally refuses to get involved. This defense is temporary in the sense that it must be used anew each time the situation calls for it. A defense used temporarily that may become permanently embedded in the ego on the basis of a persistent instinctual conflict is *reaction formation.*

The person who uses reaction formation as a defense mechanism has changed his personality structure. It is as if the danger he guards against were always present and he is now, with his changed personality, continually on guard. Anna Freud showed the formation and function of this defense in a hypothetical case where the female subject initially repressed feelings of penis-envy and hatred towards the mother. Aggressiveness or hatred in the little girl seemingly turned into feelings of excessive tenderness and concern for the mother; envy and jealousy, by means of reaction formation, turned into feelings of unselfishness and thoughtfulness for others.[7] This reactive alteration undergone by the ego shows how a defense may be constructed which takes advantage of the instinct's capacity for reversal. Instinctual demands for dirt and disorder connected with the anal stage of sexual development, for example, can be reversed by a reaction formation in such a way that a person reveals an extraordinary sense of order and a compulsion for cleanliness.

When an offensive impulse is thrown from within to the external world, then *projection* takes place. Intolerable behavior is seen in another person and felt to be outside one's own ego. Displacement, therefore, can take place both within the psyche, as when derivatives are formed, and without the psyche as in projection. This latter mechanism breaks the connection between a dangerous impulse from the id and the idea by which it would be presented to the ego by having the inner impulse perceived by the ego as if it were outside the self. The other fellow has incestuous desires, or a wandering eye, or a disturbed conscience. The defense protects the ego from the pain that would accompany self-knowledge.

Often it seems a particular defense is used more frequently than another against specific threats to the ego's security. Anna Freud writes that this kind of discrimination begins in childhood when the ego then feels the simultaneous pressures of both instinctual and external stimuli. The ego adapts to particular needs and will defend itself against internal threats to its security or will be on guard against external threats.[8] Thus, external dangers might be dealt with by denial, whereas recurrent internal impulses might be handled by reaction formations. But the ego may also combine defenses. *Undoing,* whereby an unacceptable action, affect, or thought is canceled by its acceptable opposite, may work hand in glove with *regression,* a return to an earlier stage of functioning where the ego avoided conflict.

The precise identification of any particular defense mechanism used in a given situation is extremely difficult. Generally speaking, a defense betrays itself by behavior that is not quite called for, that is not predictable, that is energetically more than or less than what one would normally expect under ordinary conditions. Since all people live with their defenses, however, which is to say, since all people live with their repressions, one comes to regard most defensive behavior as commonplace.

While not to be listed among defense mechanisms, the dream is another important outlet for repressed materials, probably the most familiar one. Defense mechanisms and dreams both function as outlets, and in addition both make the unacceptable acceptable by distortion. As the disguised fulfillment of a repressed wish, the dream distorts reality while satisfying forbidden impulses. In sleep, the repressive functions of the psyche are reduced, but not abolished. As long as the ego, which retains some awareness even in sleep, does not recognize forbidden activity going on in the unconscious mind, then a person is permitted to sleep undisturbed. Dreams induce and prolong sleep by altering the meaning of subconscious activity. If dream representatives of repressed drives reach an intensity sufficient to arouse the censoring ego, then a person awakes. The less relaxed the ego, the stronger the dream distortions must be to insure sleep.

We rely heavily upon distortion techniques when we actually tell or write about our dreams. This telling constructs a manifest dream, the dream we remember upon awakening in the morning. The latent dream we had at night contained the unconscious wish; the manifest dream disguises that wish so as to make it unrecognizable to an alerted censor. Taylor Stoehr draws upon this manifest disguise in a book entitled *Dickens: The Dreamer's Stance* (1965): "What fiction can quite reasonably imitate is the telling of dreams, which is the only conscious experience we have of them anyway (taking 'remembering' as a kind of telling to oneself)." Telling about a dream is the closest we can get to the pure dream, but the pure dream is imperfectly remembered in feelings, sensations, and pictures; an individual remembers what he cannot translate into words, and then he virtually reconstructs the dream in the telling. Stoehr uses this premise to interpret Dickens' novels as if they were his dreams: "It follows from a theory of Dickens' literary manner as a 'dream manner' that his novels may be analyzed or interpreted in the way dreams are analyzed and interpreted—that is, at once formally and symbolically, as though the incidents of fiction comprised, like those of dreams, a special kind of language, with its own lexicon and grammar."[9] Stoehr shows much of Dickens' language to be in fact a special kind of dream language.

The manifest dream condenses the latent dream in various ways: it omits elements of the latent dream; it uses fragments of the latent dream; and it makes composite images of images that appeared in the latent dream separately and distinctly. The manifest dream also displaces elements of the latent dream, for example by casual, indirect reference to something which was directly experienced, or by transferring emphasis from one thing to another. Latent dreams jump back and forth in time, and ignore spatial relationships; manifest dreams pay attention to time and space, for in the telling of the dream we consciously make the dream as intelligible as possible. Missing links are supplied, details are added or changed, even a rude plot may be invented. Dream language, therefore, is ambiguous: it has one meaning in the latent dream, and another meaning in the manifest dream. Yet disguise is common to both languages. The latent dream hides from the relaxed ego whatever is objectionable enough to arouse the ego. And the manifest dream is in itself a disguised surrogate for unconscious dream thoughts. Thus, what is sexually repressed finds expression in the distortions of dream language.

Part or all of a repressed experience, memory, or idea may be expressed in dreams symbolically. The energy attached to the repressed becomes attached to its symbol, a condition that again allows discharge by distortion. All symbols alter what they represent. The alteration is most extreme, the symbol is most difficult to understand, when the representation is related to an original which has the power to cause an individual extreme anxiety. Freud once thought all dream symbols were connected with psychic disturbances that a person experienced and repressed literally within days of his dream, but the fact that many dream symbols seemed to have little or no connection with immediate experiences led him to write on the subject with reference to a "layer of antiquity": one dreams in certain constant symbols with fixed meanings that are not individually determined but are acquired through a racial heritage. These symbols with fixed meanings appear in mythology, folklore, religion, and art as well as in dreams. From the conscious expression of symbols, Freud drew inferences as to the unconscious material behind them.

Lecture ten, "Symbolism in Dreams," from the *Introductory Lectures on Psycho-Analysis* (1916-1917), is the most important of all Freud's writings on symbolism. Here he points out that people make use of symbols without knowing about them, and even refuse to acknowledge their meaning and significance after they have been explained. Here, too, he says, "The range of things which are given symbolic representation in dreams is not wide: the human body as a whole, parents, children, brothers and sisters, birth, death, nakedness—and something else besides." The "something else besides" is a field represented by an extraordinarily rich symbolism. "This field is that of sexual life—the genitals, sexual processes, sexual intercourse. The very great majority of symbols in dreams are sexual symbols." There are not very many subjects represented in dreams, and yet the symbols for those subjects are extremely numerous. Since his interpretation of the symbols is rather narrow, frequently restricted to an explanation of their sexual meaning, Freud himself has to say, "In contrast to the multiplicity of the representations in the dream, the interpretations of the symbols are very monotonous, and this displeases everyone who hears of it; but what is there that we can do about it?"

Among the symbolic substitutes for the male organ are things that resemble it in shape, such as sticks, umbrellas, posts, and trees, or objects which penetrate into the body—sharp weapons, knives, daggers, spears, sabers, and also rifles, pistols, and revolvers. In addition, the penis is represented by objects from which water flows, or by objects capable of being lengthened. Female genitals are symbolized by pits, cavities, hollows, vessels, bottles, receptacles, boxes, trunks, and other such space enclosures. Doors and gates are symbols of the genital orifice. Breasts are represented by apples, peaches, and fruit in general. The pubic hair of both sexes is seen as woods and bushes, although the female genitals are frequently seen as landscapes.

Masturbation is indicated by all kinds of playing, as well as by gliding, sliding, or pulling on extended objects. Freud notes, "We come across special representations of sexual intercourse less often than might be expected from what has been said so far. Rhythmical activities such as *dancing, riding* and *climbing* must be mentioned here." Ladders, steps, and staircases, especially walking on them, are symbols of sexual intercourse, the common element being the rhythm of walking up them, "perhaps, too, the increasing excitement and breathlessness the higher one climbs." Another representation occurs when a key opens the door to a locked room.

After presenting material used in dream symbolism, Freud says it is incomplete and could be carried further.

> But I fancy it will seem to you more than enough and may even have exasperated you. "Do I really live in the thick of sexual symbols?" you may ask. "Are all the objects around me, all the clothes I put on, all the things I pick up, all of them sexual symbols and nothing else?" There is really ground enough for raising astonished questions, and, as a first one, we may enquire how we in fact come to know the meaning of these dream-symbols, upon which the dreamer himself gives us insufficient information or none at all.

The answer is, the meaning is learned from fairy tales, myths, buffoonery, jokes, folklore, poetry, and colloquial linguistic usage. One need only point out how these sources use the same symbolism found in dreams.

Parents often appear as royalty in dreams, which recalls the fairy tales that begin, "Once upon a time there was a King and Queen." Father and mother in fairy tales and dreams have children called princes, and the fairy King himself is father of his country. A more subtle relationship between dream symbols and their derivatives concerns birth. In dreams, birth is expressed by some connection with water: one gives birth or is born by falling into or out of water. Collectively, men evolved from aquatic creatures, stepping out of water, and individually every man is born by falling out of the water called amniotic fluid. The embryo owes its existence to this water. Freud writes, "I do not say that the dreamer knows this; on the other hand, I maintain that he need not know it." Even in the nursery, birth is connected with water: the stork, a wading bird, brings babies, and he gets the babies from a pond, or stream, or pool of water. Information about man's heritage appears in countless forms both to infants and to adults.

The dream symbol of departure as dying, for instance, need not go back to the small child's being told a dead person has gone on a journey. Shakespeare writes of the traveler who shall not return from the undiscovered country, and colloquially one speaks of "the last journey." Ancient Egyptians journeyed to the land of the dead, and Freud calls *The Book of the Dead* a kind of Baedeker the mummy takes to guide him on his journey. No individual in the nineteenth or twentieth century needs to forge for himself a meaning for the dream symbol of death.

Men use genital symbolism when they call a woman an "old bag" or an "old box"; the New Testament uses it when a woman is called "the weaker vessel." Late Hebrew literature represents a woman by a house, whose door is the vagina. Female genitals symbolized by landscapes occur again and again in mythology, where men have a sexual relationship with Mother Earth. Here is expressive symbolism which one need not even be aware of in waking life.

Freud concludes, "We can only say that the knowledge of symbolism is unconscious to the dreamer, that it belongs to his unconscious mental life." The same symbols lie ready-made for different individuals, in different ages, in different countries. The same symbols are used in dreams, fairy tales, myths, linguistic usage, and art. Freud feels that people refuse to acknowledge symbolic expression because so much of it is intimately related to sexuality. "I should not like to leave the subject of dream-symbolism without once more touching on the problem of how it can meet with such violent resistance in educated people when the wide diffusion of symbolism in myths, religion, art and language is so unquestionable. May it not be that what is responsible is once again its connection with sexuality?" In other words, people have difficulty accepting the content of their own sexual repressions, which is perhaps why they repress that content to begin with.

Defense mechanisms and dreams are the most common outlets for indirectly expressed sexuality, but there are still other outlets which allow sexual expression in disguised forms. For example, after Oedipus slew his father, married his mother, and atoned for his sins by blinding himself, he called attention to the connection between sight and sexual vitality, where blindness signifies punishment in the form of sexual weakening. Visual impressions frequently arouse libidinal excitation, and blocking those impressions, especially by blinding oneself, can be a symbolic act of castration. In scoptophilia, a kind of sexual gazing, the eye corresponds to an erotogenic zone. It is normal to derive sexual pleasure from looking, unless, as Freud points out in *Three Essays on the Theory of Sexuality* (1905), looking becomes a perversion by being (a) "restricted exclusively to the genitals, or (b) if it is connected with the overriding of disgust (as in the case of *voyeurs* or people who look at excretory functions), or (c) if instead of being *preparatory* to the normal sexual aim, it supplants it." Voyeurs and exhibitionists, those who long to substitute looking for acting, attach the same kind of emphasis to sight and sexuality as did Oedipus; the eye takes on genital significance.

Normal sexuality can also be perverted by a fetish, whereby an object entirely unsuited to fulfilling the normal sexual aim replaces the natural sexual object. It is not unusual for a man to value a material possession of a woman who sexually stimulated him, but if the woman is deeply desired, and unattainable, then sexual behavior can become pathological by the man's spending his sexual energy on the fetish as a substitute for the woman. It is one thing to say, as Goethe does in *Faust,* "Get me a kerchief from her breast, / A garter that her knee has pressed," and quite another thing to value fur as a substitute for pubic hair, or a woman's underwear as a substitute for the woman. Earrings, slippers, shoes, long hair, and braids are among the fetish symbols for men. Long pointed objects can be fetish symbols for women. The person who uses a fetish to replace a normal sexual object is often not conscious of the substitution. In *The Psychoanalytic Theory of Neurosis,* Otto Fenichel adds, "In fetishists, the possessive urge to be the sole owner of the object is particularly stressed, and some fetishists are 'collectors'; the fetish may be an object with little intrinsic value but takes on an immense importance through the fetishistic overvaluation."[10]

Just as a fetishist tries to satisfy his sexual desire by deviating from normal sexual behavior, so does a transvestite. A man dressed as a woman cohabits not with the woman but with her clothes, and the transvestite himself represents a phallic woman under whose clothes a penis is hidden. A female transvestite unconsciously makes believe she has a penis and possesses the masculinity of her father. These perversions allow sexual energy to be discharged in private acts of psychological significance.

The aim of any sexual perversion is the same as the aim of any normal sexual act: to relieve the tension or conflict caused by libidinous energy seeking release. When that energy is repressed, it stays within an individual, constantly influencing his personality and his modes of expression. Otto Fenichel writes interestingly of a specific barrier to sexual expression and a common evasion of the barrier:

An isolation that occurs very frequently within our culture

> is that of the sensual and tender components of sexuality. It is a consequence of the repression of the Oedipus complex that many men (and also quite a number of women) do not succeed in attaining full sexual satisfaction because sensuality can be enjoyed only with persons toward whom they have no tender feelings or, even, toward whom they have contemptuous feelings or none at all. "They cannot desire where they love, and they cannot love where they desire." The institution of prostitution gives men of this type an opportunity to isolate their objectionable sensuality from the rest of their life, and thus relieves them of the necessity to repress it.[11]

Conscious behavior is continually influenced by repressions, for nothing that is repressed can be willed out of the unconscious, nor can it lose its dynamic character.

As strong as the pressures were in Victorian England to force people, writers in particular, to repress sexual expression, even stronger was the power of the repressed seeking release. Sexual impulses seem to succumb to demands of cultural suppression in every age, and yet those impulses are discharged in literally dozens of ways, including each of the discharge outlets discussed in this Appendix. Art itself has at its disposal the energies of repressed sexuality. One portion of the repressed can be diverted from its immediate aim through sublimation so that the diverted energy becomes a force in artistic creation. This does not mean that art as a form of expression is necessarily sexual; it means, rather, that art can possess an amount of sexual energy which sublimation transforms and redirects. On another level, art serves as a more immediate outlet to repressed sexuality, and on this score Freud has a good deal to say.

In a paper on metapsychology, he wrote, "The artist is originally a man who turns from reality because he cannot come to terms with the demand for the renunciation of instinctual satisfaction as it is first made, and who then in phantasy-life allows full play to his erotic and ambitious wishes."[12] The artist actually participates in all that he writes about, and thus satisfies strong needs within himself. *The Future of an Illusion* says, "Art offers substitutive satisfactions for the oldest and still most deeply felt cultural renunciations." But the artist presents his material in such a way that it does not betray its origin in proscribed sources. *Introductory Lectures on Psycho-Analysis* says of the artist, "He possesses the mysterious power of shaping some particular material until it has become a faithful image of his phantasy; and he knows, moreover, how to link so large a yield of pleasure to this representation of his unconscious phantasy that, for the time being at least, repressions are outweighed and lifted by it." Other people respond to this representation from the writer's unconscious because they, too, have unconscious needs which are made accessible by art.

With reference to the artist and his audience, Freud wrote the following in *An Autobiographical Study*:

> His creations, works of art, were the imaginary satisfactions of unconscious wishes, just as dreams are; and like them they were in the nature of compromises, since they too were forced to avoid any open conflict with the forces of repression. But they differed from the asocial, narcissistic products of dreaming in that they were calculated to arouse sympathetic interest in other people and were able to evoke and to satisfy the same unconscious wishful impulses in them too.

Since the artist can transform his unconscious wishes into art, he enables us to respond to work which expresses repressed sexual wishes that live in everyone from the days of childhood. The artist dares to express forbidden impulses, but he relieves himself of guilt because he knows his audience will vicariously share his unburdening; the audience relieves its guilt by telling itself the artist is primarily responsible for uncovering forbidden material. Through art, men share the guilt of sexual expression.

Sharing the guilt, however, is not a conscious activity. The artist does not consciously express forbidden sexual material to begin with, nor does his audience consciously respond. Here, then, is where all of the psychic operations described earlier come into play. Sexual repressions are made manifest through numerous defense mechanisms and through symbolic language and behavior. The literature of any age gives testimony to this kind of communication, and Victorian literature, produced in an unusually repressive age, makes available to the psychoanalytically oriented critic a wealth of sexual communication.

Unlike the psychologist who can talk to a living person about his sexual life, the literary critic gets his information mainly from words on a page. Instead of dreams and free association, lengthy interviews and hypnosis, biographical probing and psychological tests, the critic has novels and poems. But he also knows what the psychologist knows: sexually repressed energy continually seeks release, and there are identifiable forms of such release, and the forms have significant sexual meaning. When a literary context suggests the possibility of a sexual content, then the critic is in the position of any psychoanalytic investigator. Given the raw material, he works to his best ability to understand its significance and communicate his understanding.

Notes and Sources

1: Victorian Sexual Morality

1. Jerome Hamilton Buckley, *The Victorian Temper* (New York: Vintage Books, 1964), p. 109.
2. The 1851–1853 Census report is quoted in William L. Burn, *The Age of Equipoise* (New York: W. W. Norton & Co., 1964), p. 271.
3. Gordon S. Haight, "Introduction" to George Eliot's *Adam Bede* (New York: Holt, Rinehart and Winston, 1964), p. vi.
4. Edward Palmer Thompson, *The Making of the English Working Class* (New York: Pantheon Books, Inc., 1964), p. 370.
5. Richard D. Altick, *The English Common Reader* (Chicago: Phoenix Books, 1963), p. 103.
6. "Law Against Indecent Exposure," *Sexual Offences: A Report of the Cambridge Department of Criminal Science* (London: Macmillan, 1957), pp. 357–59.
7. On the 1857 Obscene Publications Act see Burn, *The Age of Equipoise,* p. 161; G. Rattray Taylor, *Sex in History* (New York: Vanguard Press, 1954), p. 216; Alec Craig, *Above All Liberties* (London: George Allen and Unwin, 1942), p. 39; Anne Lyon Haight, *Banned Books* (New York: R. R. Bowker Co., 1955), p. 144.
8. Burn, p. 7.
9. Buckley, p. 117.
10. Altick, "The Book Trade, 1851–1900," *The English Common Reader.*
11. On Victorian views about masturbation see Richard Lewinsohn, *A History of Sexual Customs,* trans. by Alexander Mayce (New York: Harper, 1958), p. 294; Taylor, *Sex in History,* p. 223; Acton is quoted in Chapter 1 of Steven Marcus's *The Other Victorians* (New York: Basic Books, 1966).
12. Walter E. Houghton, *The Victorian Frame of Mind, 1830–1870* (New Haven: Yale University Press, 1957), p. 408.
13. See *ibid.,* p. 357.
14. Statements about inhibiting effects on literature appear in Marcus, *The Other Victorians,* p. 109; Buckley, *The Victorian*

Temper, p. 117; Houghton, *The Victorian Frame of Mind,* p. 358; Altick, *The English Common Reader,* p. 124.
15. Crane Brinton, *A History of Western Morals* (New York: Harcourt, Brace, 1959), p. 350.
16. Mark Spilka, *"The Other Victorians," Victorian Studies* 10 (March, 1967) : 295.
17. Marcus, pp. 100–1.
18. Houghton, pp. 365–66.
19. Lewinsohn, p. 292.
20. Acton is here quoted in Houghton, p. 366.
21. Sir Philip Magnus, *Gladstone* (New York: E. P. Dutton & Co., 1964), p. 106.
22. Excerpts from *Winter Notes on Summer Impressions* are translated in David Magarshack's *Dostoevsky* (New York: Harcourt, Brace & World, 1963), pp. 207–8.
23. Marcus, pp. 283–84.
24. Buckley, p. 2.
25. Mario Praz, "The Victorian Mood: A Reappraisal," *Backgrounds to Victorian Literature,* ed. Richard A. Levine (San Francisco: Chandler, 1967), p. 55.
26. *Ibid.,* pp. 56–57.

2: The Problem of Intention

1. Leon Edel, *Henry James, The Conquest of London* (Philadelphia and New York: J. P. Lippincott Co., 1962), pp. 44–45.
2. *Ibid.,* p. 44.
3. Robert Lee Wolff, *The Golden Key* (New Haven: Yale University Press, 1961), pp. 268–70.
4. Unless otherwise noted, all references to these novels and poems which will appear in my text are to standard editions.

3: Robert Browning's "The Last Ride Together"

1. William Cadbury, "A Method for Judging Browning," *University of Toronto Quarterly* 34 (October, 1964) : 62.
2. Karl Kroeber, "Touchstones for Browning's Victorian Complexity," *Victorian Poetry* 3 (Spring, 1965) : 101.
3. Robert Langbaum, "Browning and the Question of Myth," *Publications of the Modern Language Association* 81 (December, 1966) : 578.
4. William Lyon Phelps, *Robert Browning, How to Know Him* (Indianapolis: The Bobbs-Merrill Co., 1915), p. 146.
5. Edward Berdoe, *The Browning Cyclopaedia,* 3rd ed. (London:

Swan Sonnenschein & Co., 1897), p. 252; Arthur Symons, *An Introduction to the Study of Browning* (London: J. M. Dent, 1906), p. 125; Henry C. Duffin, *Amphibian* (London: Bowes & Bowes, 1956), p. 58.

6. Recent comments on "The Last Ride Together" may be found in William Clyde DeVane, *A Browning Handbook,* 2nd ed. (New York: Appleton-Century-Crofts, 1955); Irving Orenstein, "A Fresh Interpretation of 'The Last Ride Together,'" *Baylor Browning Interests,* no. 18 (May, 1961); Dallas Kenmare, *An End to Darkness* (London: P. Owen, 1962).
7. See Albert Mordell, *The Erotic Motive in Literature,* rev. ed. (New York: Collier Books, 1962), p. 124.
8. C. H. Herford, *Robert Browning* (Edinburgh: W. Blackwood, 1905), p. 139.
9. Mark Twain, *Letters from the Earth,* ed. Bernard DeVoto (New York: Harper and Row, 1966), p. 17.
10. Lona Mosk Packer, *Christina Rossetti* (Berkeley: U. of California Press, 1963), p. 113.

4: Alfred Tennyson's "Lancelot and Elaine" and "Pelleas and Ettarre"

1. Norman Cameron, *Personality Development and Psychopathology* (Boston: Houghton Mifflin Co., 193), p. 668.
2. Paull F. Baum, *Tennyson Sixty Years After* (Hamden: Anchor Books, 1963), p. 193.
3. Lawrence Poston, III, "'Pelleas and Ettarre': Tennyson's 'Troilus,'" *Victorian Poetry* 4 (Summer, 1966): 204.
4. Clyde de L. Ryals, "Eros and Agape," *From the Great Deep* (Athens, Ohio: Ohio University Press, 1967).

5: Spasmodic Poetry

1. Jerome Hamilton Buckley, *The Victorian Temper* (New York: Vintage Books, 1964), p. 42.
2. The editions I will quote from (which do not contain line numbers to the poems) are: Philip James Bailey, *Festus,* 4th American edition (Boston: Benjamin B. Mussey, 1847); Ebenezer Jones, *Studies of Sensation and Event* (London: n.p., 1843); Alexander Smith, *A Life-Drama* (Boston: Ticknor and Fields, 1859).
3. Buckley, pp. 48–49.

6: Charles Dickens; Orphans, Incest, and Repression

1. Ada Nisbet, "Charles Dickens," *Victorian Fiction: A Guide to*

Research, ed. Lionel Stevenson (Cambridge, Mass.: Harvard University Press, 1964), pp. 44–153.

2. George H. Ford, "Introduction" to *David Copperfield* (Boston: Houghton Mifflin Riverside edition, 1958), p. vii.
3. Vereen M. Bell, "Parents and Children in *Great Expectations,*" *Victorian Newsletter,* no. 27 (Spring, 1965), p. 21.
4. In George Orwell's *A Collection of Essays* (New York: Doubleday, 1954), p. 96.
5. J. Hillis Miller, *Charles Dickens, The World of His Novels* (Cambridge, Mass.: Harvard University Press, 1965), p. 121.
6. See Mark Spilka, *Dickens and Kafka* (Bloomington, Ind.: Indiana University Press, 1963), pp. 50–53.
7. For example, Jack Lindsay, *Charles Dickens* (London: Andrew Dakers, 1950), pp. 289–90; Edgar Johnson, *Charles Dickens,* vol. 2 (New York: 1952). Cf. pp. 679 and 687; Gwendolyn B. Needham, "The Undisciplined Heart of David Copperfield," *Nineteenth Century Fiction* 9 (September, 1954): 89; George Ford, ed. *David Copperfield,* p. viii; and Spilka, *Dickens and Kafka,* pp. 47, 192–93.
8. George H. Ford, ed., *David Copperfield,* p. viii.
9. Spilka, p. 47.
10. F. R. Leavis, *The Great Tradition* (New York: Doubleday Anchor Books, 1954), p. 288.
11. Daniel P. Deneau, "The Brother-Sister Relationship in *Hard Times,*" *The Dickensian* 60 (Autumn, 1964): 173–77.
12. Monroe Engel, *The Maturity of Dickens* (Cambridge, Mass.: Harvard University Press, 1959), p. 136.
13. Robert Morse, *"Our Mutual Friend," The Dickens Critics,* ed. George Ford and Lauriat Lane, Jr. (Ithaca, N.Y.: Cornell University Press, 1961), p. 208.
14. K. J. Fielding, *Charles Dickens* (Boston: Houghton Mifflin Co., 1965), p. 227.
15. Angus Wilson, "The Heroes and Heroines of Dickens," *Dickens and the Twentieth Century,* ed. John Gross and Gabriel Pearson (Toronto: University of Toronto Press, 1962), p. 10.
16. Bell, "Parents and Children in *Great Expectations,*" p. 21.
17. Steven Marcus, *Dickens: from Pickwick to Dombey* (New York: Basic Books, 1965), p. 32.
18. Edgar Johnson, *Charles Dickens* 2: 679.
19. George Ford, ed., *David Copperfield,* p. x.
20. In "Little Nell Revisited," *Papers of the Michigan Academy of Science, Arts, and Letters* 45 (1960): 427–37, Mark Spilka relies

heavily upon Jack Lindsay's *Charles Dickens* (London: Andrew Dakers, 1950).

21. George Orwell, "Charles Dickens," *A Collection of Essays* (New York: Doubleday Anchor Books, 1954), p. 106.
22. Mario Praz, *The Hero in Eclipse in Victorian Fiction,* trans. by Angus Davidson (London: Oxford University Press, 1956), p. 127.
23. Spilka, p. 47.
24. Taylor Stoehr, *Dickens: The Dreamer's Stance* (Ithaca, N.Y.: Cornell University Press, 1965), p. 168.

7: Charlotte Brontë's *Villette*

1. See Elizabeth G. Gaskell, *The Life of Charlotte Brontë* (London: Everyman edition, 1960), p. 365.
2. Miss Brontë's letters appear in Gaskell, *ibid.,* pp. 365–67.

8: George Meredith's *The Ordeal of Richard Feverel*

1. Lionel Stevenson, *The Ordeal of George Meredith* (New York: Scribner, 1953), p. 71.
2. L. T. Hergenhan, "The Reception of George Meredith's Early Novels," *Nineteenth-Century Fiction* 19 (December, 1964): 219.
3. John W. Morris, "Inherent Principles of Order in *Richard Feverel,*" *PMLA* 78 (September, 1963): 334.
4. C. L. Cline, "George Meredith," *Victorian Fiction,* ed. Lionel Stevenson (Cambridge, Mass.: Harvard University Press, 1964), p. 348.
5. Quotations in my text are from Lionel Stevenson's edition of *The Ordeal of Richard Feverel* (New York: The Modern Library, 1950). Stevenson presents the complete 1859 version of Meredith's novel.

9: Psychologically Oriented Criticism

1. See Donald A. Stauffer, ed., *The Intent of the Critic* (Princeton, N.J.: Princeton University Press, 1941).
2. See Ronald S. Crane, ed., *Critics and Criticism* (Chicago: University of Chicago Press, 1952).
3. Helen Gardner, *The Business of Criticism* (London: Oxford University Press, 1963), p. 75.
4. Leslie Fielder, *Love and Death in the American Novel* (Cleveland: Meridian Books, 1962), p. viii.
5. *Ibid.*
6. Norman N. Holland, "Psychological Depths and 'Dover Beach,'" *Victorian Studies;* Supplement to vol. 9 (September, 1965): 5–28.

Appendix

1. All references to Freud's work unless otherwise noted are to the Standard Edition of *The Complete Psychological Works of Sigmund Freud* translated under the general editorship of James Strachey (London: The Hogarth Press and The Institute of Psycho-Analysis, 1953–66). Quotations in my text accompanied by specific titles will have no further documentation.
2. Otto Fenichel, *The Psychoanalytic Theory of Neurosis* (New York: W. W. Norton & Co., 1945), p. 148.
3. Sigmund Freud, "The Unconscious," *Collected Papers,* trans. Joan Riviere, 4 (New York: Basic Books, 1959): 109.
4. Anna Freud, *The Ego and the Mechanisms of Defence,* trans. by Cecil Baines (New York: International Universities Press, 1946), p. 193.
5. *Ibid.,* p. 47.
6. Grete L. Bibring, "Glossary of Defenses," Appendix B to "A Study of Pregnancy," *The Psychoanalytic Study of the Child* 16 (1961), 62–71.
7. *The Ego and the Mechanisms of Defence,* p. 51.
8. *Ibid.,* p. 191.
9. Taylor Stoehr, *Dickens: The Dreamer's Stance* (Ithaca, New York: Cornell University Press, 1965), pp. 69, 91.
10. Fenichel, p. 342.
11. *Ibid.,* p. 156.
12. Freud, *"Papers on Metapsychology," Collected Papers* 4: 19.

Index